T0300736

Songs and Recipes: For Macho Men Only

Bernie Keating

authorHOUSE®

AuthorHouse™
1663 Liberty Drive
Bloomington, IN 47403
www.authorhouse.com
Phone: 1-800-839-8640

First published by AuthorHouse 10/18/2010

ISBN: 978-1-4520-5002-7
ISBN: 978-1-4520-5004-1
ISBN: 978-1-4520-5003-4

Printed in the United States of America

This book is printed on acid-free paper.

ONE: CRACKERS AND MILK

It was car radio, air-conditioning, and seat belts that started American family life down the road to oblivion. Until those inventions, a car ride was a shared family togetherness.

> *With someone like you,*
> *A pal so good and true,*
> *I'd like to leave it all behind*
> *And go and find* [1]

Dad sang heartedly as he steered our Model A Ford down the gravel road, wind blowing in through the open windows. Mother sat in front and we five kids shared the crowded backseat and two windows with wind in our face.

> *A place that's known to God alone*
> *Just a spot we could call our own*
> *We'll find perfect peace where joys never cease*
> *Somewhere beneath the stary skies.*

> *We'll build ...*

"Bernard, stop bothering Billie and behave yourself," scolded Mother without even looking over her shoulder. How did she know I was taunting my little brother because I wanted his place next to the open window? "... and Edwin, you're not too old to sing with the rest of us. Now behave yourself and sing."

It was a Sunday afternoon drive to Hot Springs to see a movie, the first one for the summer. We had no movies in Buffalo Gap, except in the Grange Hall when the soap salesman came to town and showed horse racing movies projected against a sheet hanging on a wall; but those movies weren't that great because he kept interrupting them with commercials to sell his soap. Horse races were interspersed with soap suds.

But this afternoon we were headed to a real movie in a real theatre and the stars were my Dad's favorites, Nelson Eddy and Jeanette MacDonald in their 1936 hit, *Indian Love Call*. ... and if Betty didn't get carsick and delay us, we'd be early enough to get the best seats in the front row. It promised to be a great afternoon.

> *We'll build a sweet little nest*
> *Somewhere out in the west*
> *And let the rest of the world go by.*

A car came down the road toward us. "Here comes a car. Quick, roll up the windows!" shouted Dad as he interrupted the song. The dirt road stirred up a cloud of dust, and rolling up the windows was a small price to pay for clean air, and then down again to let it back in.

It was a great movie. On the ride back home to Buffalo Gap, I fell asleep curled up in the back seat. I dreamt I was wearing the bright red coat of the Canadian Mounted Police, like Nelson Eddie. With his rich baritone, he was singing to Jeanette MacDonald, and echoes of the song were reverberating off the mountain peaks

2

When I'm calling you – Oo Oo Oo
Will you answer too – Oo Oo Oo
That means I offer my love to you
To be your own. ...

Perhaps my words were not the same since I couldn't remember them exactly from the movie; but no matter, Jeanette was listening and smiling at me. I heard her beautiful soprano response to my song.

You belong to me,
   I'll belong to you.

Back home that night for supper sitting next to Dad, it was my favorite bedtime snack, a big bowl of crackers and ice cold milk. With our new electric refrigerator, we always had milk that was fresh and cold. A second bowl, then to bed, and dreams of my song to Jeanette. Those were sweet dreams.

Changing a flat tire, Denis is concerned that we will be late for the movie. This second photo was made in 1933 shortly after arriving in Buffalo Gap when we were dressed for dinner at a neighbor's across the street.

The B W Keating family.

TWO: WHEN IRISH EYES ARE SMILING

When Irish eyes are smiling,
Sure 'tis like a morn in spring
In the lilt of Irish laughter
You can hear the angels sing,
When Irish hearts are happy
All the world seems bright and gay
And when Irish eyes are smiling,
Sure, they steal your heart away. [2]

I am Irish, although my father refers to our family as "shanty Irish". I think that means we came from the "other side" of the railroad tracks along with the Italians and Polish.

My great-grandfather was born in County Wexford in Ireland in 1825. While he considered himself pure Irish -- like all good Irishmen do -- that is somewhat fiction because most of their ancestors arrived on the Irish Isle from somewhere else. The Celtics originated in the Caucasus Region of Central Europe and migrated westward during the early centuries. These fierce warriors conquered and populated much of Europe with their bloodline, including France, England, and the Irish Isle. In France, after some cross-breeding, they gradually assumed the identity of Normans. Later during the twelfth century, the warlike Normans conquered their Celtic cousins in England and the Irish Isle. The Irish Celtics absorbed the Normans into their culture, who then adopted the Gaelic language. One of the Norman warriors took a beautiful Celtic lass as his wife, and his name was gaelicized by her as "Ceitinn." A few centuries later when the Gaelic language gradually became corrupted with the barbaric English language, the name "Ceitinn" became "Keating". That is enough information about ancient Irish history.

Like everyone else in Ireland during the 19th century, my great-grandfather was a potato farmer. Unfortunately, a potato blight developed that turned potatoes black, making them poisonous, and causing much of the Irish population to die from starvation. Those that could, fled the island to live elsewhere by whatever means possible, the most common being by cattle boats normally utilized to transport cows to faraway places. He climbed aboard a cattle boat destined for America, along with hundreds of others who huddled in the darkened bottoms of ships where cows were normally kept. Also crowded in the bilge of that same ship were Mister and Mistress O'Rork and their two small sons. Mister O'Rork did not make it; he died at sea, and his body was thrown overboard. Mistress O'Rork arrived on the pier in New York, a beautiful widow, penniless and with two small sons. What was she to do? There on that same pier stood the Keating bachelor. What could he do? Of course, he did the only thing a decent guy could do: he proposed marriage on the spot. She accepted, and they moved to Sandusky, Ohio, where he began working in a factory rolling Cuban cigars.

To this union of Keating and O'Rork were added three other children, including my grandfather. As he grew to manhood, he got a job as driver of a horse-drawn wagon and delivered milk around the neighborhoods. When Granddad was about the age of thirty, he met and married a beautiful Irish lassie. Oops, I'm wrong. She was beautiful, but her father came from Wurtenberg, a region in what is now Germany in the area between Baden and Bavaria. For anyone to leave that beautiful area and move to Sandusky, Ohio, they must have been desperate. The lady that Granddad married, my grandmother, "tarnished" the Keating pure Irish bloodline with German blood. There is only one photo that remains of her, and she was indeed beautiful, and even looks somewhat Irish. Who knows? From this marriage came two sons: my father and Elmer, his younger brother, who was more-or-less the black sheep of the family.

At an early age, my grandmother died from what was diagnosed in those days as "consumption." I don't know what that was, and since they were too poor to see a doctor, I suspect they did not know, either. After her death, Granddad took his sons to the Black Hills of South Dakota where he went to work in a gold mine owned by the rich geezer named Gira that his sister had married. With a touch of nostalgia, Gira named his mine Cuyahoga after the county in Ohio where his home was located. The gold mine was on Iron Mountain near the Rushmore ranch, where huge granite formations carved with the faces of four presidents could later be seen. In his youth my dad hunted deer on the Rushmore ranch.

Dad was seven years old in 1899 when he arrived with his father at the Cuyahoga mine. He became a hillbilly and roamed the mountains with his rifle to bring food to the family table. School was done on the fly. He attended school by horseback in Keystone, other times in Custer, and his classroom education ended at the sixth grade. Then as a teenager, Dad worked in several gold mines. He attended a business college in Rapid City, learned something about accounting, and then began a banking career that was to extend for forty six years. When he was teller in Newell, a lovely young lady named Ethel, who was cashier at a local store, went to the bank to make daily deposits at his teller window. They were married and had four sons, including me, and one daughter

Dad had some rocky times in banking. The bank in Camp Crook closed in the aftermath of the 1929 financial crash, and Dad found himself unemployed while living in one of the most desolate, isolated regions in America with a wife and five small children. Leaving Mother and us kids with her parents in Newell, he went to school again in Rapid City to learn how to sell insurance. One day he heard about an opening at the bank in Buffalo Gap. Dad went down, was hired, had a banking job again, and the family happily moved to Buffalo Gap.

People were desperate during the Great Depression of the 1930s. Most able bodied men in town were unemployed until Roosevelt's WPA and CCC programs came along. Nobody had any money, and it was the same in every town in South Dakota. Unemployment was twenty percent nationwide and much higher in South Dakota. Banks failed overnight and people lost all their savings. When my dad started his banking career in 1918, there were forty-eight banks in the six counties of the Black Hills. By the time of World War II, thirty-three of them, or 68% had been liquidated.

I also had a banking career that started during the Depression when I was still a pre-teen. I neglected to mention who the young janitor was who climbed out of bed at five on cold winter mornings to run to the bank through snow drifts to fire up the pot-bellied stove and warm the bank for his banker father and customers when they arrived. Guess who got that job? That was the beginning and end of my banking career.

My mother was raised in a German family and everyone else in Dakota was either German or Scandinavian; so their ethnic fare was what everyone ate and the only things the grocery stores carried. It was meat and potatoes cooked in an iron skillet and served with no fuss by busy (and relatively impoverished) people. I never heard about wiener schnitzel or sauerbraten until I was an adult and encountered it as a tourist in Germany.

Nor did our family ever have traditional Irish cuisine -- if there is such a thing? Growing up we never had potato bread, fish and chips, nor even corned beef and cabbage for Saint Patrick's Day. You want to know our Buffalo Gap victuals when I was growing up? It was meat, potatoes, vegetables, and apple pie for dessert.

There's a tear in your eye and I'm wondering why,
For it never should be there at all.
With such power in your smile,
Sure a stone you'd beguile,
And there's never a teardrop should fall,

When your sweet lilting laughter's
Like some fairy song
And your eyes sparkle bright as can be.
You should laugh all the while
And all other times smile,
So now smile a smile for me.

The only photo we have of Dad's mother, who was my Grandmother. She died in her 20's from "consumption" in the 1890s, and is buried in Sandusky, Ohio. What a beautiful girl.

THREE: PORKCHOPS AND APPLESAUCE:

I don't have any nostalgic feelings for that old kitchen range we had in Buffalo Gap. All it ever represented to me was a lot of hard work and misery from my mother.

"Bernie, the wood pile is empty; go out and chop some wood, and fill up the wood box in the back porch."

"Bernie, shake down the ashes in the range so we can have supper, and take them out, and dump the garbage bucket too."

"Bernie, start a fire in the range for supper. Use some pitchy kindling; I am cooking pork chops tonight so I need a hot fire."

The only good thing was we were having pork chops tonight, and Mom did know how to make them real good. But feeding wood to that old range, and then taking out the ashes was a pain that seemed to keep me busy for most the day: a fire for breakfast, a fire for lunch at noon, and then another fire for supper in the evening.

Every kitchen in Buffalo Gap had a range. It was for cooking a meal, warming the kitchen in the winter (but made it too hot in the summer), and for heating water. Made of cast iron, they stuck out four feet from the wall and were six feet wide, so took up a lot of space for most kitchens. The range did one other thing after we got running water to the house. Dad converted the pantry behind the kitchen into a bathroom, piped the water through the back of the range, and we had hot water for the lavatory in the bathroom; but there was not enough room for a bathtub. Mother still gave us our bi-weekly bath in a washtub in the middle of the kitchen with water heated in a boiler on the range.

The garbage bucket on the floor beside the kitchen sink was no blessing for me either. In Buffalo Gap, everyone had to dispose of their own garbage. Our neighbor, Bill Sewright, with his ranch across the road from us, fed all of his wife's kitchen garbage to his pigs. He had a couple dozen hogs in a pig pen down below the hill out of sight and out of the wind currents, and for good reason -- it smelled. He dumped all his garbage in troughs where the pigs slopped it up: coffee grounds, potato peels, left-over pancakes, sour milk, and anything else Mollie wanted to get rid of that was edible to a pig, which was just about anything. His pig pen smelled like Hell warmed over. If you wanted to really insult someone in those days, the standard taunt was, "You smell worse than a pig pen!"

We had no pigs, so we dug a six foot deep hole in the back yard near the outhouse and dumped all our garbage there. Then to help contain the smell, when I had to carry out the ashes, I would carefully spread it over the top of the garbage to hold down the smell. It seemed to work okay, at least for our sensitivities of the time. Everything and everyone had some sort of odor.

The wood requirements were not so easy. Chopping big blocks of wood with an axe into kindling small enough so it would fit in the range was hard work. When I did it for Grandma Sewright or Grandma Dalbey, I was paid twenty-five cents a rick. At home I was paid nothing. In fact, at home it was a negative, because I would be blamed if the wood box was empty, or if the wood was split too big to burn good, or too small, wet, or not pitchy enough for whatever was going to be cooked. "Bernie, we are out of wood, the wood box is empty; get busy."

And starting a fire; now that took some skill. I'd crumble some newspaper under the wood, but it had to be an exact amount. Too little, and wood would not catch fire; yet too much paper hindered creating a good draft, and created more ashes to take out. Then there was the matter of pitch. You had to be able to read the pitch content of the wood and select the right stuff depending on what was to be cooked for supper. Steak required a very hot fire, but that didn't happen often because we seldom had steak. Pancakes would go well with bigger pieces of wood and less pitch. If mother was baking homemade bread in the over, then you did not want to get the range top too hot, so go for pithy wood that burns slowly and for a long time. Like I said; selecting the right wood took some skill.

Now tonight, we're having pork chops; so that takes wood somewhere between baking stuff and a hot steak fire, and since pork chops get finished in the oven, bear that in mind.

I must say Mother was a good cook; in fact, she was a very good cook. Pork chops was one of her specialties. We didn't have it all that often, mostly a few times in the fall after Bill Sewright butchered some of his hogs. Many years later, after Dad had died and Mother was visiting our family in California, I asked her if she'd make us some pork chops for supper. She agreed, and I must say, they were the best pork chops I'd had since those suppers back in Buffalo Gap.

My wife, Aurdery, who is also a good cook, kept an eye on what Mother was doing and wrote down the recipe. Since then, Aurdery also does a great job with pork chops. Maybe not quite as good as mother's, but close.

The first thing is to select the right chops. They can't be fancy. I've made the mistake of selecting some better ones, more expensive cuts, thicker cuts, but they never are as good. Chops have to relatively thin and have the evidence of some good fat. That's a requirement for good pork chops.

Start with a bread board, rolling pin, and crackers. Spread out the crackers and grind them into crumbs with the rolling pin, the smaller the crumbs the better. Whip up an egg and pour it on a flat plate. Pour some cooking oil in a frying pan and get it hot. Use a lot of oil, because it will be drained off later. Dip each pork chop in the egg, lay it on the cracker crumbs until both sides are well coated, and then place it in the hot oil. Only about three chops will fit in most frying pans, four if they are small.

Now use a spatula and when the bottom side turns a golden brown, about two minutes, turn it over. Don't overcook in the frying pan because that job will be completed in the oven. A casserole dish should be pre-heated at 325 F and the bottom coated with butter. Pick the chops out of the oil in the frying pan and place in the casserole dish.

Now, here is a secret my mother had almost forgotten that Aurdery noticed. With a teaspoon, ladle some cream over the top of each chop. That will add a rich flavor and keeps the pork chops more moist as they spend the final 15 minutes in the oven.

You cannot have pork chops without its companion -- a dish of applesauce. Enjoy.

Our family in 1967 when we lived in Portland and were about to move back to California. We moved six times during my 50 year business career: Oakland, Portland, Moraga, Palos Verdes, Toledo, and back to California.

FOUR: A NICKEL CANDY BAR

"How much do you charge for splitting a rick of wood?" asked the old lady who stood in her doorway facing me.

"Twenty five cents a rick and I split it into small pieces so it will burn real good in your kitchen range, and I stack it too, nice and straight; so it's easy for you to pick up and haul into the kitchen," I replied. At eight years of age it wasn't easy for me to make a sales pitch to a total stranger. I knew she was Grandma Sewright, who lived down the street all by herself; she was the mother of Bill Sewright, who ran the ranch across the road from our home. I liked Bill, but I'd never talked to her before, and anyway I was shy around strangers.

"That sounds like a fair price. Are you sure you can chop it so it burns good?"

"Yes, Ma'am," I replied with as much enthusiasm as I could muster for a total stranger, and an old lady at that. "And if you've got some blocks with knots and a lot of pitch in them, I'll cut it extra fine and keep it stacked separate for you to use when you've got meat to fry that needs high heat from that old range. And I'll cut up a few blocks into really small stuff for you to use in the mornings to start a fire."

"That's good."

"And if I find some pithy blocks of wood, I'll stack that wood aside so you can save it for when you're baking bread in the range oven and need a slow heat."

"Good. I see you've split wood before, and know how to do it."

"Yes, Ma'am, I split wood for Grandma Dalbey all the time. You can ask her. She'll tell you I do a good job, and I charge her the same twenty-five cents a rick." In truth, that wasn't much pay for splitting a rick of wood and placing it in a stack four foot high and eight feet long, but these were the Depression times of the 1930's, and it was about the only spending money a kid could make. Twenty-five cents would buy me five Power House candy bars at Mel's Service Station, enough to last me a week, one per day. Mel Thompson had just opened up his new station to sell gas for cars, and he also sold bottles of pop and candy bars -- a new thing for him after closing his livery barn during the past year. Few ranchers or cowboys rode their horses into town anymore, and those that did just hitched them under a shade tree somewhere. Sometimes I'd help my big brother deliver the weekly Chicago Sunday Tribune on Wednesdays after the train arrived, and we could keep three cents out of every dime the paper cost; with twenty customers that was sixty cents my brother split with me. So I was able to keep myself supplied with candy bars and an occasional bottle of pop, and still save some money for the future. Those Power House candy bars were about the only big luxury I had in Buffalo Gap.

It was hard times. Even though my dad ran the bank and everyone in town thought we were rich, he only made fifty dollars a month, and that was only a dollar more than most other fathers in town made from working on the WPA -- only they also got crates of oranges and their kids got warm snow suits for the winter, while I got nothing -- only the patched hand-me-downs from my big brother.

"And I supply my own axe," I said as a final clincher. "My big brother keeps it nice and sharp."

"Okay," she said. "You are the little Keating boy, aren't you?"

"Yes, Ma'am, I'm Bernard. I'd rather be called Bernie, but that's what Mother calls Dad, so that name is already used up."

"Okay, Bernard," she said as she smiled. "Twenty five cents per rick, and I think one rick is about all I will need done. When you finish, knock on my back door for your pay. Maybe I'll even have a glass of cold milk and a piece of angel food cake for you."

The deal was closed, and it was a good deal with some income for me and a fair price for the old lady.

That was the occasion when I first met Molly Sewright, who I always knew as Grandma Sewright. Little did I realize, nor even care, that she was one of the first white women in the Black Hills. Everyone in Buffalo Gap seemed to be a pioneer, so no big deal. Her father was a Union Army General who served during the Civil war under General Grant and when the war ended he was honorably discharged. Three years after arriving in the Black Hills, the General died. Mollie was being courted by William Sewright and married him that same year. After marriage they lived as ranchers in the Buffalo Gap area. A cave behind the ranch house served as a hiding place where Mollie would flee with her children during Indian scares, while her husband mounted his horse and joined fellow ranchers in a band of home-guard militia riding hard after the Indians. During the uncertainty of those early days, there were many panics.

Bill Sewright was Mollie Sewright's son. His ranch house, barn, and horse corrals were across the road from where we lived, and we looked out our front door at his barnyard. I spent most days of summer over there playing with his grandson, and we shadowed "Pop Bill" everywhere he went. The previous year, his only son had been drowned in a flash flood, so he seemed to welcome the constant companionship of two young boys. Or at least, if he did mind, I never heard about it. During the summer, I would saddle up a horse and drive his herd of milk cows to and from their pasture which was several miles east of town.

In July, he'd take his mother, Grandma Sewright, and us kids camping. He'd load the back of his pickup with a tent and camping stuff. Grandma Sewright would sit in the cab in front, and we kids would sit in back on the gear while Pop Bill would drive us to the old Sewright ranch. He helped set up the tent, then he'd leave, and we'd spend a couple nights camping. Grandma Sewright did the cooking over a camp fire in an old iron skillet that came with her to the Dakota Territory in the stagecoach. Around the campfire at night, Grandma Sewright told us how it was to be a bride living in the Dakota wilderness, and how scared she got when the Indians came though during the uprising. Grandma Sewright was in her seventies when we went camping and seemed awful old to be doing that sort of thing. Funny thing; now that doesn't seem so old any more. I am now in my eighties, still tent camping and cooking over a campfire with an old iron skillet.

Bill Sewright exposed us to the Indian culture. Each winter he'd kill some old milk cow that stopped producing and butcher it in the barn with us kids watching the process. Some winters he would also kill a couple of hogs and some sheep. Then he'd take them out to the reservation. He didn't actually sell anything, because the Indians were destitute. It was a bartering process: he would trade in return for their agreement to come to his ranch during the summer to work off their debts. Besides the No Water family who took up residence in tents by Beaver Creek, Francis and Sylvia Stanz and their two children lived across the street from us in an abandoned rail boxcar Sewright had moved onto his property. Some of the men who came without their families slept in a hay barn. John Sitting Bull was there; a deaf mute in his seventies when I knew him in Buffalo Gap, was a teenager at the Battle of the Little Big Horn. His father was the famous Chief Sitting Bull. John was a tall, austere-appearing man who projected great presence -- even with his silence -- but he was kind to us kids and let us ride with him when his team of horses and wagon moved out into the hay fields. Comes-Again and Pursey Kills-A-Warrior were others I knew who had fought against Custer, and Sally Spotted-Bottom was a teenage girl in the Little Big Horn encampment at the time of the battle.

Bill sometimes took his grandson, Billy, and I along on the bartering trips to the Indian reservation. I suspect it made for a more respectful image and safe journey with a couple kids in tow rather than traveling alone. The meetings always began with *HOW-ko-dah*, which was a respectful hello. Later in the bartering process the definitive phrase was when the Indian asked *mah-zah-SKA E-cha-zo*, -- how much do I owe you? I was never sure Bill was a fair trader: a cow that died of old age and some potatoes given to a starving Indian family in mid-winter in return for a summer's work on his ranch, but he was more charitable than the U.S. Government.

Children of the Lakota who came to Buffalo Gap became my playmates. I was *pah- HA SAH-pah*a *hok-SHE-lah*, a Black Hills boy. George No Water and I rode our stick horses around the neighborhood and through the ranch. Sometimes we were permitted to saddle up and ride real ponies. In a boyhood custom of that day, we made small cuts on our wrists and held them together in a symbolic exchange to become blood brothers. He became part white, and I became part Lakota.

When I delivered the *Chicago Sunday Tribune* in Buffalo Gap during the 1930s, there was a comic strip named "Alley Oop," and it had a professor character who invented a time machine that could transport you back to some unique time and place in history. If I can find that professor in real life and his time machine, I will ask him to send me back for a visit to the Bill Sewright ranch in Buffalo Gap so I could have another conversation with those elderly Indian friends of mine

Unfortunately, that time machine can do nothing for the price of my nickel candy bar. It now costs me $1.85.

Denis, me, and Edwin having fun in our play yard in Camp Crook.

My sister, Betty, on a swing in front of our home in Camp Crook. When the 1929 crash came, our home went into default and we lost it. For a few months we lived with our grandparents in Newell, and then Dad got the job as Cashier of the Buffalo Gap State Bank. For the next twenty years we lived in rented houses. It was in Edgemont in 1950 before my parents decided to purchase a new home.

When my Mother and I visited Camp Crook in 1989, we found the house had been moved across the Little Missouri River to a farm, where it was used for a granary.

FIVE: *SONG OF SITTING BULL*

I-ki-di-ze wa-on-kon
He wa-na he-na-la-ye-lo
He i-yo-ti-ye ki-ya-wa-on

A warrior
I have been.
Now
It is all over.
A hard time
I have. [3]

George No-Water, Billy Thompson, and I rode our ponies down the ravine to Beaver Creek, waded across it with the water knee deep to the horses, and entered the No-Water encampment at the edge of the cottonwood grove on the Sewright ranch. The Sioux grandfather, reclining against a log in the shade alongside the teepee, watched as we dismounted and turned our horses loose. The old man, wearing a solitary eagle in his hair which hung long and straight, smiled and said something in Sioux to his grandson.

"What did he say, George?" I asked.

"He said in the old days when they lived here with Sitting Bull, he had a pinto mare exactly like yours. He's always talking about the old days and the crazy things they worshipped. It's boring. Come on; let's go over to the hay barns and play."

George and Billy were my playmates for the summer. I lived in Buffalo Gap, a town named for the valley that created a passage for the buffalo into the Black Hills. The Pine Ridge Indian Reservation was a few miles east on the Dakota prairie. My family lived across from the Sewright ranch, and I spent most hours of the summer over there with his grandson. As a struggling rancher barely keeping his head above water during the rough depression years of the 1930s, Sewright hustled any way he could. One of his enterprises was to butcher cows during the winter time and take them to the Indian Reservation to sell. He didn't actually sell anything, because the destitute Sioux had nothing. It was a bartering process. He'd give them meat, and they agreed to work summers on his ranch where he'd supply them with food and a place to stay. The Stands family spent the summer living in an abandoned rail box car that had been moved to the vacant lot across from our house. Their two children were playmates of my younger sister and brother. Several Sioux: Percy Kills-a-Warrior, Comes-Again, and John Sitting Bull, would come without their families and live in an abandoned hay barn. The No-Water family pitched a tent alongside the creek that meandered through the ranch. George No-Water's father drove a team of horses to pull mowing machines during the haying season.

The grandfather, I never knew if he had a first name we just called him No-Water, was an old man in his eighties, long past the age of working on the ranch. He sat all day in the shade under the cottonwood trees. While he understood some English, he seldom spoke anything but Sioux, and I learned some of it. When we boys struck his fancy, he would tell us stories about the old days. Often I'd linger with him alongside the campfire, someone to listen to an old man with many memories about life on the prairie that no one else wanted to hear.

No-Water had been raised a member of Sitting Bull's tribe that had roamed this country as nomads, living in teepees, and following the buffalo herds. This gap in the mountains was their camping place while the buffalo herds were leaving the Black Hills with the first snows and moving onto the plains where the snowdrifts were lighter. The Sioux pitched their teepees here near the gap and feasted on the plentiful buffalo. Then later in the winter, the tribe would move with the meandering herd out onto the plains and hunker down in protected ravines, sheltered from the blizzards that blew around the north end of the Black Hills.

No-Water was a survivor. He had been with Sitting Bull at the Little Big Horn when Custer attacked their village. That was sixty years earlier when he was a teenager. It was a confused battle with women, children, warriors, and soldiers everywhere. After the battle, he fled with Sitting Bull into Canada. A dozen years later after he had returned to the reservation, he was with the Sioux at Wounded Knee. His family was slaughtered by the United States Cavalry as he watched helplessly from a nearby ridge. He married again, and his grandson was my playmate.

His stories came across the campfire as the old warrior turned hunks of meat on the crude spit. This night he felt like talking, and it came with a combination of Sioux and his blend of English. I understood most of it; George translated the rest.

"Did he ever go up into the Black Hills when he was a boy?" I asked. The answer was a resounding no! The Black Hills was a hostile place where few Indians ventured except in an armed hunting party; it was full of bears and other prey that attacked them and spooked their horses. Then there was the thunder and lightning. The old warrior's eyes closed as he mumbled something. He had once climbed the mountain we call

Bear Butte where he was close to those Spirits; he saw visions of the White Buffalo. A cloud came, thunder roared, and lightning struck the trees; then he fled down the mountain in a rain storm, never to return. He was telling me of the Vision and these Spirits as he turned the spit over the fire. Then George's father returned from his day on the ranch and told me I must go home before my parents worried, because a storm was on the way.

The storm hit. Lightning bolts off the high peaks turned night into day, thunderclaps shook the foundations of our house, and then the rain and wind uprooted trees that crashed to the ground outside my bedroom window. These were No-Water's angry Spirits, and I could believe in them just as I did in the white man's church-God I heard about on Sundays. Was No-Water's vision of a White Buffalo -- his symbol of hope -- a God? I had my own dreams, too. Perhaps we each search for our White Buffalo.

The cowboy Bill Keating

My oil painting of Chief Sitting Bull. I knew his deaf, mute son, John Sitting Bull, who worked summers on the Sewright ranch and was always friendly to us Keating kids.

Another of my oil paintings, General Custer. If you love the Rambo movies, you would have appreciated Rambo's twin, the ultimate action hero of his day.

SIX: THE SMELL OF BACON

I was excited! Everybody loves bacon and pancakes, especially over a campfire. This was my first Boy Scout hike, first time cooking over a campfire, and first time in the bowels of wild Calico Canyon.

Calico Canyon was a deep recess where prairie suddenly runs up against steep cliffs and the Black Hills begin. My home town, Buffalo Gap, sits alongside the little creek that flowed down from the mountains; but you probably never heard of Buffalo Gap -- it wasn't much even as South Dakota towns go -- only one hundred eighty seven people, and seven of those were my own family.

Yes, it was a small town, but we had a great Boy Scout troop, and I was a new tenderfoot with my sights already set on becoming an Eagle -- just like my brother. It was the biggest thing in my life. Hiking across the prairie, we saw a coyote looping across a rise and down into a ravine. Then we reached the bottom of the cliffs and headed into the canyon. There were only deer trails to follow, and the climbing was tough. It was wild country. I had laid in bed many nights listening to the scream of mountain lions from up here, and their tracks with the claw marks were along the trail. Tonight, I would be camping with those big cats as my neighbor, and my eyes searched the woods on all sides.

I carried a sack slung over my back with a frying pan, food, and jug of water, hatchet, and a blanket. In the 1930's, we had no mess kits, canteens, sleeping bags, or fancy things like that -- at least no one in Buffalo Gap had them.

The scoutmaster picked a campsite, and the older scouts made a pine bough lean-to in case of rain, but if it was a clear night we would be curled up in our blankets under the stars.

First came supper. We gathered small firewood for cooking and bigger logs for the campfire after dark. With the help of another scout and two matches, I got a fire going. I was hungry, threw a slab of bacon into the frying pan and held it down over the flames. It started to sizzle, and then splatter.

… and it was nearly a disaster. I did not know you had to cook bacon slowly. "Bernard, raise the frying pan higher," warned my big brother. "Bacon has to be cooked slowly, otherwise it will all burn up." I learned my first lesson in cooking over a campfire: know when to cook slowly and when over a hot flame.

Now for the pancakes. They were a standard bill of fare for our family during the 1930s -- either for breakfast or supper. We hungry brothers needed lots of cheap fuel to keep our legs moving during those years of the Depression, and we may not have survived except for Aunt Jemima's pancake flour. It was ideal on a scout hike for the same reason, and every scout learned to mix the batter and cook frying-pan size cakes.

We bought the pancake flour and most groceries at John Degnan's store. Buffalo Gap hasn't had a grocery store for fifty years, but back in those days before the town dried up, we had three: Phillips, Towers, and Degnan's. Since my dad was the town banker, he had to patronize all three and pass his business around -- what little our family had available to pass. Mother baked bread, we got fruit and vegetables from the orchard and garden, and Mother spent most the summer canning and filling Mason jars for the long winter ahead.

We got milk from the Bill Sewright ranch next door. Bill had eight milk cows and a bull, which he pastured a mile east of town. I'd usually saddle up his horse, Buck, and herd the cows to and from pasture, and even help with the milking during the summer. Bill Sewright did not need the milk from the cows for drinking -- it was for the cream that came out of the separator. Cream was Mollie Sewright's money crop, and the left-over skim milk was a nearly worthless by-product. So our family always had plenty of cheap milk, and what we didn't use, Bill Sewright would feed to his hogs. With five kids, our family drank a lot of skim milk.

We needed a hot fire for the pancakes, so I threw on small limbs with pitch, placed the frying pan down close over the flames, and poured in enough batter for one pancake. It sizzled great and when bubbles started to form on the topside, it was time to flip it over. That's where my brother came to my aid. He demonstrated with our first pancake. First, he un-stuck the pancake from the pan by swishing it back and forth. When it was free, he jerked the pan upward and the pancake went flying though the air above the pan. With the skill of a juggler, he caught the cake with the uncooked side against the hot pan. Now down over the fire again to cook the other side. Using a jackknife, you peek under the edge and see when it turns a golden brown.

Wow! Bacon and pancakes, and my first scout hike; it doesn't get any better than that, but I sure hope that mountain lion is quiet tonight.

We sat on logs around the campfire and told stories and sang scout songs. I grew sleepy. When the sun sank below the high cliffs and darkness crept in, we knew it was time to call it a day. The scoutmaster formed us in a circle with our arms on the shoulders of each other, and we sang the song that had been sung around campfires for decades. It was the refrain of taps.

Day is gone.
Gone the sun,
From the plains,
From the hills,
From the sky.

All is well.
Safely rest,
God is neigh.

The coyotes down on the prairie were signing to the moon, but that mountain lion was quiet. Knowing God was neigh, I felt secure. Crawling into the blanket, I fell asleep before I even remembered to count the stars.

Boy Scout troop in Buffalo Gap in 1940. I was only 11 and not eligible to become a tenderfoot until I was 12. Edwin is center back, Denis on right in back, and I am lower right. Photo taken at time Denis became Eagle Scout on way to Mt Rushmore where the ceremony was held.

We are a scouting family. Eagle scouts above are me, Ari Dimas, Roger, and Deke. George Dimas is Assistant Scout Master. Photo was taken on Christmas Day 2006.

SEVEN: WASHDAY-MONDAY SOUP

I've been working on the railroad
All the livelong day.
I've been working on the railroad
Just to pass the time away.

Can't you hear the whistle blowing
Rise up so early in the morn.
Can't you hear the captain shouting
Dinah, blow your horn.

This song is as old as anyone can remember, and no one knows where it came from. While its origin is unknown, there are several versions of its history. The one I like best is that it is an old hymn adapted by Irish work gangs in the West. That fits rather well with the Keating gang in Buffalo Gap (and most other families in the town) on Washday Monday. The day was a traditional family affair that rivaled that of a railroad work gang.

In the 1930s, our family water supply was rainwater that fell on the roof and drained into a cistern under the back porch. A hand pump fed water into a bucket for drinking, and a tea kettle on the stove supplied warm water for all the other uses. The cistern water was not particularly flavorful for drinking because of a decided taste of cedar shingles; but it was not "hard" water and about as "soft" as water can be, since it fell from the heavens, so it was excellent for washing clothes on Washday-Monday.

Early Monday morning, Dad pumped a five-gallon boiler full of water and heaved it onto the kitchen range over a hot fire. After breakfast before he left for work, he and Mother together carried the heavy boiler of hot water to the back porch where the Maytag washing machine sat waiting for its big moment, and they carefully poured the scalding hot water into the tub. Then Dad left for work at his job running the Buffalo Gap State Bank, and Mother and our gang of five Keating kids took over.

It was a procedure we kids knew well, and each had a job to do, which varied over the years as older brothers gradually moved into retirement and the younger ones took over. Mother organized the clothes into piles starting from the cleanest -- Dad's white shirts for working in the bank -- then pillow cases, then sheets (except for those of Billie who wet the bed), then mother and Betty's clothes, and finally ending up with boys dirty trousers and smelly socks.

Then we kids took over, throwing each batch into the tub in the order Mother had provided. I was the "tub" man. After each batch had swirled back and forth for about 15 minutes, I turned the lever for the tub to "off" and the wringer switch to "on". The Maytag wringer consisted of two spring-loaded rubber rollers that squeezed together and pressed the water out of the clothes as they were fed through and dropped into a tub of rinse water. Feeding the wringer was my favorite job. Using a stick, I grabbed a garment and fed it into the wringer, pulling the stick back before it was caught. Using a stick was important because it saved bruised fingers if they should be caught with the clothes going through the wringer. The Maytag had a quick release if this happened, but after making the mistake of slow reaction and pain, one soon learned to use a stick. Then the wringer was swung into a new position between the rinse tub and an empty basket to catch the finished product.

At that point, Mother took the wrung-out clothes outside and hung them on the clothes line attaching them to the wire with a clothes-pin. After my older brothers were tall enough, they were coerced, under protest, into clothes-line duty.

If it was summer, the clothes would be dry by Tuesday and ready for folding. If it was winter, when temperatures were often below freezing, the clothes would be frozen as stiff as boards and must be brought in close to the stove to thaw-out and hang on racks in the dining room until dry.

Wednesday was Mother's ironing day. Dad always wore a white shirt (and necktie) to the bank and to church on Sunday, and mother had to sprinkle starch onto them and then carefully iron. Pillow cases and sheets must also be ironed, although with less care. Ironing was accomplished with a detachable flat iron that was heated on the range stove, and then placed into a handle for the job. The work for us kid was finished on Tuesday, and by Wednesday evening, Mother's weekly clothing chore was completed, and she could turn her attention to ridding-up the house for the weekend, and a few other things she had to do such as cooking three meals a day, etc., etc., etc..

Back to Monday; there was not enough time for Mother to prepare our usual big noon meal, which we called "dinner" and the lighter evening meal was called "supper", so Monday was "soup day". Our standard bill of fare on that day was Washday-Soup, which I always loved, but could not recall how it was prepared. Many years later I phoned Mother for the recipe. Her memory was a bit fuzzy from old age. She said, "Put butter in a skillet, pour in some flour, brown it, pour in a mash of potatoes and milk, and stir while heating." I tried that, but my version was not very good. I think she forgot some cooking embellishments that for her were almost automatic.

So I began to re-create the soup as I remembered it. This may be a corruption of Mother's, or it may be the same, but now I call the recipe "Washday-Soup @ Bernie."

Here is how I prepare it.

1. Carefully clean 3 large leeks and one large onion, chop finely, and add to a skillet with 3 tbs. of canola oil. Sauté over low heat for 5 minutes (or a bit longer), slowly adding 3 cups of chicken broth.
2. Peel and dice two large potatoes and boil in 3 cups of chicken broth for 15 minutes (until potatoes are tender), and then mash the potatoes.
3. Pour #1 into #2.
4. Stir in 3 tbs. of gravy flour.
5. To #4. add ½ bunch of finely chopped parsley, 3 stalks of finely chopped celery, salt, paprika, and 2 cubes of beef bouillon.
6. Add a package of chopped pastrami.
7. While covered, bring to a slow rolling boil for 20 minutes, then taste and add whatever else is needed to make it your own creation.

Alas!! I have managed to recreate Mother's washday soup, and it tastes even better today when I know I do not face an afternoon of running that Maytag wringer.

> *Someone's in the kitchen with Dinah*
> *Someone's in the kitchen I know*
> *Someone's in the kitchen with Dinah*
> *Strumming on the old banjo, and singing*
> *Fie, fi, fiddly i o*
> *Fie, fi, fiddly i o*
> *Fie, fi, fiddly i o*
> *Strumming on the old banjo*

Me, Billie, and Betty. I remember posing for this picture with a travelling photographer who set-up shop in the upstairs of Mime's Inn in Buffalo Gap. I don't recall the struggle to wear a bow tie, but I see I did not get it on straight. Bill looks to be about two, so this is probably in 1935

EIGHT: ONWARD, CHRISTIAN SOLDIERS

Onward, Christian soldiers, marching as to war,
With the cross of Jesus going on before.
Christ, the royal Master, leads against the foe;
Forward into battle see His banners go!

Since my religion of record is Roman Catholic, it takes some explaining why a Protestant song is one of my favorites. It gets complicated.

My father, whose mother died when he was six, moved from Ohio with his widowed father to a remote gold mining camp in the Black Hills of South Dakota, a dozen miles from the nearest town. Far from any church, they knew little of organized religion, but in the Irish tradition, they called themselves Catholic and clung to that faith.

My mother lived in the farming community of Newell, was raised a Methodist, and her father was a deacon in the Methodist church. It was boring to be a girl in a family that did not permit card playing, dancing, or much of anything else, and required them to spend a good part of Sunday in church.

Dad got a job as teller in the Newell bank, the same town where Mother was a cashier in the local dry goods store. Every day, she had to visit the bank and make a deposit at the window with the handsome teller. Some days she found the need for several such visits. One thing led to another, which led to a proposal of marriage by the Catholic guy to the Methodist lady.

Her father, the Methodist deacon, was not very happy with the prospect of having a Catholic son-in-law, but what could he do? Nothing! They were married and immediately left for the groom's new assignment at a bank in Camp Crook, eighty miles away in a remote region of northwestern South Dakota with dirt road that were often impassable. Mother made one visit a year with us kids to Newell, but her parents never did make it to Camp Crook.

Any religious differences the newly married couple encountered were trivial, because there was virtually no organized religion in Camp Crook. A building with a cross overhead was designated as a Catholic church, but was simply a local adornment because no priest was ever assigned and the building was rarely visited except by a travelling missionary. The building designated as a Protestant church also had a checkered history. It was originally funded by a charity from the East as an Episcopal church, but later closed due to declining membership, then reopened as Methodist, then later closed again as money and congregations ebbed and flowed.

After ten years in Camp Crook, my parents, now a family with five kids, moved to Buffalo Gap, and felt it was time for some religion. Since Mother had pledged to Dad at the time of marriage that any kids would be raised as Catholic, we became Catholic. There was a Catholic church building in Buffalo Gap, but no priest had ever been assigned to the parish, and services were held only once a month by a missionary priest from Hermosa, forty miles to the north. There were less than a dozen people in the congregation, and some of them came only at Christmas and Easter. My older brothers were indoctrinated sufficiently to become Altar Boys, and we children were forced to remain in the pews after the conclusion of Mass where the priest grilled us on the Baltimore Catechism.

On the Sundays when no priest came to town, Mother took us to the Methodist church. Reverend Hatfield worked as a carpenter during the week and since he was an ordained minister, he conducted Sunday services to help the Methodist congregation gain their passport to Heaven. Prior to his service, we kids attended a Sunday school class where we learned about the Saint James Bible.

I loved those Methodist services and particularly the singing. Everyone sang with gusto, no one needed a hymnal, we were marching, marching, marching, and everyone seemed happy and glad to be there. I loved it.

> *Onward, Christian soldier, marching as to war.*
> *With the cross of Jesus going on before.*

Those Sundays in the Catholic Church were not so great. For one thing, in summer the place was stifling hot and in winter was freezing cold with only a potbelly stove with heat barely reaching the second pew. The second pew was where our family of seven sat with Mother admonishing us to be quiet, and Dad mostly looking bored. We were reminded to sit quietly, except when it was time to stand or to kneel and pray. My prayers were for a quick end to Mass. If I ever had a genuine religious experience in that church, I don't remember when it was.

At Christmas time and again at Easter, the priest insisted we have a choir and music. The choir consisted of Mother, Julia Stands-Alone, a beautiful Indian lady from the nearby Sioux reservation, my younger sister and brother and me. Mother pumped the foot pedal on the organ and sang. Julia was a beautiful singer. My younger siblings could barely read and mostly mumbled, and I lip-synched. The songs were nothing I had ever heard before or liked. It mattered little that the music was sub-par, because there were usually less than a dozen people in the church, but we had a choir and music and the priest was happy.

When I grew older, I was pressed into service as an altar boy to relieve my older brothers who begged to retire. With services only once a month, my training for the job was minimal. During the Epistle, which the priest mumbled in Latin, I had to keep my eye on his left heel. When he raised it, it was my signal to go up on the altar and carry the heavy missal from the right side to the left side of the altar. Then later at another signal from the priest, carry the missal back again to the right side. It was no big deal, except that sometimes I tripped on my long cassock when climbing up the altar steps.

My most important duty as an altar boy came near the end of Mass. In those days, the priest had to fast with no food or water from midnight until after his last Mass of the day. He started at 7am with his first Mass in Hermosa, then drove twenty miles for his second Mass in Fairburn at 9am, and then travelled another twenty miles for our 11am Mass in Buffalo Gap. So by the end of our service, he was reeling from hunger and thirst. My job was to leave the church, walk a block to Mel's Service Station at the corner, order a cup of coffee, carry it back, and place it on the left side of the altar. Since I was attired in a cassock, Mel knew my mission was for charity; so there was never any question of paying for the coffee. After the priest finished the last gospel, he took a big swallow of coffee, and then turned to give the final blessing to the congregation.

After the services were concluded, came the part of those Sundays I liked best. The priest was a fun guy, and he always came to our home for a breakfast, it then being almost noon. And what a breakfast feast we had. There were fried potatoes with gravy, scrambled eggs, toast with lots of butter, cheese, milk, applesauce, and sometimes sausage. We kids were cautioned beforehand to go light in loading our plates so there would be plenty left for the priest, but we knew Mother would not scold us in front of company; so we heaped it on. It was great.

In the religious culture of my youth, I learned the Saint James Bible in the Methodist Church and the Baltimore Catechism in the Catholic Church. I learned to sing with gusto in the Methodist Church, and how to carry the missal and serve coffee in the Catholic Church. I don't remember doing much praying in either place. There was no confusion in mixing the two religions, because they were the things you did on Sunday. During the week, you did stuff because it was the right thing to do.

> *Onward, Christian soldiers, marching as to war,*
> *With the cross of Jesus going on before.*
>
> *Onward then, ye people, join our happy throng,*
> *Blend with ours your voices in the triumph song.*
> *Glory, laud and honor unto Christ the King,*
> *This through countless ages men and angels sing.*

Mother and Dad dressed for church in 1942. At that time, Dad was working in Edgemont bank and Mother in the Buffalo Gap bank; in December the family moved to Edgemont.

Mother's Lewis family of Newell; and not a smile among them; they just returned from Methodist Church services. Front row: Granddad, Ethel (my mother), Vera, Grandma. Back row: Blanche, Bessie, Clarence, and Claude. The two boys fought in World War I. My mother lived to be the oldest at 97 when she died. I love her bonnet with the fancy bows; she was stylish even back then.

The stair steps: Denis, Edwin, Bernard, Betty, Billie

NINE: REMEMBER PEARL HARBOR

Let's remember Pearl Harbor
As we go to meet the foe.
Let's remember Pearl Harbor
As we did the Alamo [4]

I am sure you remember November 11, 2001 when terrorist crashed planes into the World Trade Center in New York City and created an inferno which killed three thousand people. I also remember Pearl Harbor Day, December 7th 1941, when Japanese planes attacked Hawaii with nearly the same loss of life. That "day of infamy" was the beginning of World War II for the United States of America.

I was twelve years old, living in Buffalo Gap, and playing with my best friend, Dick Sewright, who came over from Hot Springs to visit his grandmother. Dick and I were exploring the back alleys and playing make-believe war games -- cavalry against the Indians. When we went to the Sewright ranch house for a drink of water, we found all the adults huddled around the radio listening to a flash news report. Unidentified planes were dropping bombs on Pearl Harbor. Maybe they were Japanese? Who are the Japanese and why were they dropping bombs on Hawaii? Where was Hawaii?

The adults were glued to the radio and talking in frightened tones, but it was exciting and a mystery to Dick and me, We returned to the alley, but now our war game was shooting at Jap planes. We were suddenly in a real war and knew the enemy was Japan. Who are the Japs?

Looking back seventy years later, I can still feel the hysteria that swept the country in the aftermath of that day. The make-believe war games of Dick and me took on a new dimension. We were now in a real war and American men would be killed in combat -- already had been at Pearl Harbor. We organized the defense of Buffalo Gap and planned how we would repel those Japs if they came charging down from out of Calico Canyon into the outskirts of our town. This was not a make-believe war; it was for real. I was in charge and would lead the defense of Buffalo Gap..

The measures that Dick and I took to defend our town were duplicated nationwide with air-raid drills in cities across the country. In Buffalo Gap, the town leaders organized our defenses and conducted drills. My dad was an Air Raid Warden and his duty station was in our neighborhood which included the Bill Sewright horse corrals and barns across the street from our house. When the sirens on the fire station rang to announce the drill, all the lights in town were turned off, blankets were hung in every window, and we kids huddled in darkness. I've often wondered what the Sewright's horses thought when they heard those wailing sirens and found themselves in total darkness. Horses spend the night standing up, so perhaps they slept through the whole thing.

But those times were no laughing matter and only the beginning of five long years of wartime, and those years were to consume my entire high school career. All young men between the age of 18 and 38 were drafted and conscripted into the military service. After boot camp was completed, most were sent overseas into combat. Many young women headed to California to work in aircraft factories or in shipyards. Buffalo

Gap was drained of population with ranchers and farmers about the only people left. During the 1930's we had listened to the music of Glenn Miller at Saturday night dances in the auditorium, but now they were seldom held and when they were, it was with old men playing fiddles and elderly dancers limping to songs from World War One. Living in Buffalo Gap had become depressing.

Military service and wartime combat became very personal to families. In our immediate block, we had seven men and women in military service. My two brothers were in the navy with the oldest in the North Atlantic fighting German submarines. Ed Streeter, next door, was in the navy flying planes off an aircraft carrier and fighting Japanese in the South Pacific, and his brother, Victor, was in Europe fighting Germans through the hedgerows across France. Norman Bondurant, my buddy from next door, was in the Seabees and killed on Iwo Jima. His sister, Helen, was in the WACs (Woman's Auxiliary Corps). Margaret Sewright, from the ranch across the street, was an army nurse caring for the wounded on a hospital ship in the South Pacific. A small flag with a silver star representing each service man hung in the window of their homes. We had two silver stars in our front window for Denis and Edwin. In the Bondurant home there was a silver star for Helen and a gold star in memory of Norman.

Everyone had a ration card. It seemed nearly everything was rationed: tires for cars, meat, sugar, butter, and gasoline. New cars did not exist for six years, not that anyone had much gasoline to go anyplace. It was difficult to find toilet paper in our local grocery store; we survived using scraps of newspaper. If you wanted to travel to Hot Springs, you would hitchhike and hope someone with gasoline would pick you up. Picking up hitchhikers was considered patriotic. At the age of fourteen, I often went to Hot Spring using my thumb.

We kids played make believe war games. I was the oldest in our group, so I organized an army. I appointed myself a corporal and was in charge. My younger sister and brother, plus Billie Thompson and Bill Bain, were all assigned the rank of PFC. We fought the enemy through the horse corrals and vacant lots on the Sewright ranch and up and down the alley behind our house. After the first week of the summer, the troops grew restless, so I promoted myself to sergeant and all the rest to corporals. The real war dragged on and also our make believe wars. A year later I was a major general and had promoted everyone else to brigadier general and gave each a certificate to prove it. I can show you mine in my scrapbook where it is with my high school and college diplomas.

Buffalo Gap virtually died as everyone moved away to some sort of wartime job. My family moved to Edgemont so Dad and Mother could assist the bank in the boom-time that developed as the U.S. Army established an ammunition depot on the prairie south of town. I was in the 8th grade and attended classes in the afternoon, because the school was divided to make classroom space and handle the influx of children of defense workers. We remained living in Edgemont for the duration.

After three combat tours on a destroyer in Korea, I can state that war is not fun.. They are also an extremely difficult and stressful time for the civilian population on the home front. Since Pearl Harbor day, we Americans have a lot of wartime experience. It seems that for the past seventy years we have always been in a war or on the brink of a war. After the end of World War II, within less than five years we were back again in combat in Korea. Then a few years later we were drawn into the Vietnam War that went on for years amid great controversy on the home front. I lose track of short conflicts in Panama and Granada. Then came 9/11 and the wars in Iraq and Afghanistan which are still being waged. I wonder what our country would be like today if we had not spent all that treasure paying for wars and if we still had all the young Americans who lay buried around the world in military graveyards?

Perhaps we are fortunate that World War II began with Pearl Harbor when we had no alternative but to fight. The most difficult decisions have been those that begin in controversy; why are we there? How do we extricate ourselves from such conflicts? What is the exit strategy? Those kinds of wars create internal dissention that turns the country into armed camps of opposing opinions. That certainly happened during the Vietnam War with the turmoil of the 1960s and again to a lesser degree in Iraq and Afghanistan.

The country entered the Korean War at the time when it was still tired from fighting World War II, and many questioned why we were shedding the blood of young men again half-way around the world in a foreign country few could find on a map. After spending the first of my three combat tours in Korea, I returned home and people asked where I had been. They scarcely knew a war was going on and, in fact, it was not even a declared war; it was only a United Nations police action.

In our modern era, this all began at Pearl Harbor. The theme that quickly developed was "Remember Pearl Harbor". I do remember that day, and I also think about the decades of wartime since then. Maybe some time in my lifetime I will enjoy a country that is neither at war nor on the brink of war; but I doubt it. That may be too much to hope for.

Headlines for the day after Pearl Harbor, and this was the day President Roosevelt delivered his speech "A Day of Infamy," as he stood before congress and asked for a Declaration of War.

TEN: *YOU ARE MY SUNSHINE*[5]

You are my sunshine
My only sunshine.
You make me happy
When skies are grey.
You'll never know, dear,
How much I love you.
Please don't take
My sunshine away.

I never had any "girl friends" during my pre-teen years when I lived in Buffalo Gap. It is not that I did not have eyes for a couple girls, but I was too shy to ever follow the lead of my heart. In addition to the problem of shyness, there was also the embarrassment of teasing by my big brothers. At the first indication I might be sweet on someone, I'd hear, "Bernard has a girl friend, Bernard has a girl friend, Bernard has a girl friend." I don't know why the teasing since they never had any girl friends either, and maybe that is the reason. While I was "sweet" on girls at different times in grade school, it was an un-expressed love, because those girls did not have a clue to my yearnings.

There was one exception when my heart ran over, and it was during the 7th grade end-of-year school picnic up in Craven Canyon. A tradition was to hold a class picnic on the last day of school. It was not a big event since there were only six in my class, four girls and one other boy. It was decided we'd hold our picnic in this deep canyon that was ten miles from town. Joe Bennett had a small ranch where Craven Canyon opened up into a wide meadow and a meandering stream trickled through. The creek was usually dry by the end of summer, but in the spring it had a good flow.

Bill Sewright, who was also the unofficial town mayor, agree to drive the class to and from the picnic in the back of his pickup truck. It had high sideboards for use when hauling cattle to market; so it was ideal for a herd of students standing in back.

We loved the wind rushing past our faces and girls' hair blowing free in the wind as Sewright drove down the rutted road; the pickup swayed back and forth. After six miles, we left the dirt road and headed up the trail that lead to Craven Canyon. Now the pickup was bumping and swaying so hard that we had to hang onto the side boards and each other to remain standing. It was great.

So there were the teacher and six students with a full day ahead, and the meadow all to ourselves. What to do? I decided we should start by exploring the ravines that led into the canyon, and everyone followed me. After an hour finding nothing of interest, we decided it was time to eat. The girls spread blankets on the ground, opened the baskets, and laid out the picnic lunch. I love picnics. I guess I have eaten at five hundred of them: Mother's Lewis family reunions every year in Sturgis, Catholic picnics in Hermosa, Methodist picnics at the Game Lodge, Odd Fellows picnics in their vacant lot; but the best were our own family picnics at Blue Bell. Ladies who organize picnics always try to think of something new to include, but the menus were always the same: fried chicken, deviled eggs, potato salad, dinner rolls, and baked beans. Then depending, on the season, there would be either watermelon or ice cream. For a school picnic in the spring, watermelon was out-of-season and ice cream was not in the cards; so we had cookies the girls made instead.

The pace slowed down after lunch and the girls sat around chatting. I decided to be on my own and engage in my favorite picnic activity, which was to build a rock dam across the small creek. I walked to the creek and surveyed it for the best place for a dam. I waded into the water, which was ankle deep, and began to lift rocks into place. Soon, who should wade in beside me and begin to lift rocks into place but Eileen Egger.

I was sweet on Eileen; she was pretty with beautiful long hair that fell over her shoulders. We had a great time lifting those rocks and dropping them into place, and a couple times she helped me with heavier rocks and we did the job together.

It wasn't long until the other guy, Darrell Thompson, showed up and waded into the water. I knew he was also sweet on Eileen; here he was trying to beat my time. I could tell I had the upper hand because Eileen moved even closer to me and we began to work together, even on the smaller rocks. When the other girls showed up, they just sat on the bank and watched.

By the time the Sewright pickup returned and it was time to go, we had built a great dam. It was ten feet across and held back the water three feet deep. Eileen nearly stumbled as we climbed out, and I caught her hand so she wouldn't fall. She kept her hand in mine, and we walked together to the pickup. My heart was racing fast.

In the back of that pickup on the way to town, I knew I had found a "girl friend." The road was bumpy and the pickup swayed back and forth. Eileen and I had to hold each other so we could keep standing on our feet. That's when we began to sing, the wind blew her hair in my face, and we smiled at each other.

> *You are my sunshine*
> *My only sunshine..*
> *You make me happy*
> *When skies are grey.*
> *You'll never know, dear,*
> *How much I love you.*
> *Please don't take*
> *My sunshine away.*

The wind rushed past, we held hands, and sang at the top of our voices to each other. All six classmates were there, but I had eyes only for Eileen.

That was the last time I ever saw her. Her father had struggled during those Depression years and had been waiting for the end of school so they could move to Oregon.

I never hear that song that I don't think of Eileen. That was seventy years ago. I wonder what kind of life she had? I hope it was a good one.

The railroad bridge swimming hole. It had been a mere twinkle of a stream until a flood in 1938, then it became eight feet deep; we spent most summer afternoons there.

ELEVEN: THE DAYS OF WORLD WAR II

That all I longed for long ago was you
... That all I longed for long ago
Just one look and then I knew
That all I longed for long ago was you [6]

The haunting voice of Jo Stafford is coming from the juke box as I stand in the cafeteria lunch line. It is the summer of 1945. Germany has surrendered, but World War Two continues as we face the invasion of Japan as our next challenge. I am a high school sophomore, working ten hour days and seven days a week. I get wages of $1.25 per hour with time and a half over eight hours per day and double time on the weekends; I am earning $125 per week

As a teenager I already had three years of working experience by the age of fifteen. With all the men in the service, young women working in California aircraft plants, and older people already with jobs, there was work for anyone. After the 8th grade and freshman school years finished, I worked digging ditches for the city of Edgemont. The next summer I worked on a survey gang for the Department of Geodetic Survey, who were mapping the land in eastern Wyoming that had never previously been surveyed. The next summer, I worked on the Igloo Black Hills Ordnance Depot. I made concrete sidewalks, and then became a "skilled" roofer, building roofs over racks of bombs. I laid asphalt shingles on hot tar and nailed them on a roof built thirty feet in the air above racks of bombs.

Don't look for it on any map, but there was once a city in South Dakota named Igloo. Its name came from the bomb cellars that resembled the snow hut of the Eskimo. Igloo was a real town, too, with over four thousand people, elementary and high schools, churches, hospital, and a movie theater; all these were enclosed behind a seven foot fence where a badge with your picture was required for entry. Armed guards patrolled the fence line. This government town on the Black Hills Ordnance Depot was named Igloo

When World War Two started, the army needed a place to stockpile ammunition in advance of D day. The prairie sage brush country in the southwest corner of South Dakota was selected for an ammo depot. My hometown became a boom town as the nearby army base was being built, and Edgemont grew overnight from a few hundred ranchers and railroaders to 10,000 construction workers who occupied every building and shack; many slept in tents and cars. The line to cash a payroll check extended out the side door of the bank and around the corner. Cafes and saloons played to packed houses. Illegal poker games flourished in the back room of a dozen saloons.

At the same time that workers were building concrete bomb bunkers, other workers were constructing the infrastructure of a government community: barracks, duplexes, Quonset huts, churches, schools, PX, and a movie theater.

Jobs were available for anyone with minimal qualifications because all the young men were in the army. Men who had been working on the WPA during the depression years, found these new jobs were a Godsend. Government recruiters went to the Pine Ridge Indian Reservation and enticed many Indians to move to Igloo. This was their opportunity to move from poverty on the reservation, and it also became a melting pot experience. The government built a multi-denominational church. Catholic Mass was celebrated on an altar; thirty minutes later a Protestant minister started his service at a podium.

My father and mother spent one day each week at the ordnance depot operating a mobile bank that moved from bunker to bunker where they cashed the payroll checks of the ammunition handlers.

When trainloads of bombs arrived, they were stacked in the concrete bunkers. Despite the unusual mission, Igloo gradually became a normal town where people went to school, to the movie on Saturday night, and to church on Sunday. My Edgemont High School basketball team played Igloo, and a traditional rivalry developed. Igloo had excellent schools with the best facilities and equipment that the federal government could buy on short notice during a war. Tom Brokaw of TV fame started his schooling there in the Igloo grade school. His photo is in the 1947 yearbook. It was an isolated community, but few complained because those were the war years. Gas, tires, sugar, meat; it seemed everything was rationed.

One day the crews were loading ammo shipments round the clock, and we knew that D day and the invasion of Europe was at hand. Most everyone had a brother, husband, or son overseas waiting to fight onto a beachhead, so few complained of the long hours and hard work. It was a time of high emotion.

The war ended; the base was closed. All the workers were discharged and they packed belongings and moved away. Many were Indian families who moved back to the Pine Ridge Reservation from where they had come only a few years before.

The base was dismantled. The buildings were all torn down; the movie theater, church, school, and commissary disappeared; and all the barracks and family duplexes were disposed of. Alas! Even the concrete sidewalks I had built were bulldozed. At last there was nothing left except for the empty bunkers. For a time these were used in a pig feeding operation, but who needs a thousand pig feeding cellars in barren South Dakota? The operation went bankrupt. At last, the prairie returned to sage brush. Coyotes moved back and reclaimed their territory.

Last year I returned to Edgemont for a visit and drove out to see where Igloo had been. The fence lines that had been patrolled by armed guards were gone. I was hoping to find the remains of one of the sidewalks or roofs that I had built, but nothing was there except for the hundreds of empty bunkers that dot the prairie to the horizon. A lone coyote loped across the landscape. I pondered what an archaeologist of the third millennium would think when they excavate the site in the bitter cold of this remote region. Were these igloos of a legendary Eskimo tribe?

Igloo is a forgotten remnant of World War Two, and is also a faded memory of my war-time teenage years.

Denis was an electrician on an aircraft carrier in the North Atlantic hunting Nazi submarines. Edwin was an instructor in electronics and radar at the Monterrey base in California.

I spent three years on the destroyer, USS Boyd, DD 544 operating in Korean waters during the Korean War. Will was drafted and spent two years at Camp Carson in Colorado where he became a specialist in mountain warfare

TWELVE: YES, I WAS ONCE A COWBOY

Oh give me a home
Where the buffalo roam
And the deer and the antelope play

Where seldom is heard a discouraging word
And the skies are not cloudy all day.

Home, home on the range ....

The song describes the 7-11 ranch, where I worked as a cowboy. We had buffalo, deer, antelope, and lots of sunshine. The ranch, on the dirt road between the towns of Buffalo Gap and Hot Springs, filled the 24,000 acres between the two towns. Most of the pastures were in high country and not accessible by road.

I was raised in the ranch environment of Buffalo Gap, where our house was adjacent to the Sprague ranch and across from the Bill Sewright ranch. We looked across the dirt road at the Sewright horse corral, where my favorite horse would usually be standing at the fence looking in my direction. Every summer, starting when I was about eight, I would saddle Buck and drive Sewright's eight milk cows and bull to a pasture a mile east of town. Then in the late afternoon, I would saddle up Buck again and bring the herd home. If I was lucky, they would be waiting for me at the pasture gate, but sometimes I'd have to ride for an hour to find them out of sight at the bottom of a ravine. They liked to aggravate me. Although I did a lot of riding during my youth, I was not an official cowboy when growing up.

That was to change the summer I graduated from high school. During World War II, I had worked on the Army Ordnance Depot as a cement worker and roofer; making good money: $120 per week. During my senior year, the war ended, the depot was closed, the GI's came home looking for work, a recession set in, and no jobs were available for anyone. I already had a NROTC scholarship to college, but still wanted to make more money. I heard the 7-11 ranch had jobs available, so I became a cowboy.

Like most other cowboys, I would not become rich. My wages were a dollar per day and room and board. My room was a cot in the bunkhouse with six other cowboys, and my meals were at the kitchen table with the other hands.

Ranch work is hard work. I would get up at 6 a.m. and head out to do the morning chores which consisted of using a pitch fork to throw down hay for a couple calves in one corral, for a dozen bulls in another, twenty heifers in a third, checking the water in all the troughs, and then head to the barn to feed oats to a team of work-horses. After all this was completed, it was time for breakfast in the kitchen of the big house. We had bacon, eggs, pancakes, fried potatoes, and baked beans, plus coffee. The cook fed us well in preparation for a hard day's work, just like I had done with the work horses.

Then started the day's work. I'd like to claim we strapped on our holsters and headed up to the high country just like the Cartwright brothers, Joe and Hoss on the TV Bonanza series. That might happen every couple weeks, but that vision is mostly Hollywood. Ranch life was far less glamorous; a temporary summer employee is at the bottom of the labor pool. I spent some days shoveling horse manure into a wagon and hooking up a team of horses to drive out to a pasture and spread the manure. Those days were easy because I was on my own and set my own pace. On other days I was haying. A haystack team consisted of four guys: a sweeper, who delivered the hay from the field to the stacker; a stacker, who used a tractor to lift the hay over the hay stack; and two guys on top the stack, who used pitch forks to spread the hay out to the edges so the finished stack would be straight and ready for the winter's weather. I was usually the guy on top of the stack where the hay, and occasional rattlesnakes, came tumbling down on top of me. It was a dirty job with no shade and was done in the heat of the South Dakota sun with temperatures of 106 degrees. The burlap water bag was always nearby.

Another job was not as tough because you got to ride on the back of the hay baler, feeding wire that will encapsulate the hay into bales. The machine was pulled by a tractor, which kicks up a cloud of dry hay dust that turns you black by the end of the day.

At noon, we ride a jeep back to the ranch house for lunch, which is another big meal in preparation for a hard afternoon of work. Then came a short rest on the cot in the bunk house, and back to the haystack. At 5 p m we'd return to the ranch and start the evening chores, a repeat of work in the corrals. After a shower and clean shirt, we'd head to the ranch house kitchen for a big supper of steak, potatoes, corn, tomatoes, beans, and pie for dessert. The steak was from range fed stock that hung briefly in the dairy shed to be "cured." We developed strong jaws after a summer of eating that meat.

We'd play pool after supper on a pool table in the middle of the bunk house. By the end of the summer, we were all pool sharks. Games were short. To determine who would shoot first and get the break, we lagged to the far cushion and the closest earned the break. We were so good at pocketing a ball on the break and nearly clearing the table, that the game was often decided before the second guy got to shoot. There was never any betting, but it was a matter of pride to be identified as the best shot in the bunk house. I often was.

The ranch had a nine man crew. Tom Judge, who had worked there for many years, was the foreman. Four other cowboys were ex-GI's recently out of the army. That included the Jenson brothers, Carl and Walt, who did most of the riding up in the mountain pastures, and Tex McPherson and Ted Hanson, who were just hanging around looking for some better job elsewhere. Tex eventually became the county sheriff, and Ted simply disappeared. The rest of the crew were recent high school graduates working during the summer and waiting to go to college in the fall. After college we all had successful careers: Dick Sewright was a dentist, Don Eibert was a naval aviator, and Tom Brown was a music teacher. Since that was the era of the universal draft, after college we all spent time as officers in a military service.

There were some fun days on the ranch. Several times during the summer we saddled up and rode to the high country where I earned the moniker of "cowboy". We left before sunrise, climbing the rocky trail through a ravine that led to the pastures in the high country. After rounding-up a hundred head of cattle that had become scattered during the summer, we herded them in a westerly direction down through several ravines into a pasture near Hot Springs, where they would winter. Then we had the long ride back to the barn, arriving home after dark. Working on a hay stack or riding a hay baler did not prepare me for the back of a horse. By nightfall, I was walking stiff and bow legged, just like the cowboy I had become.

I never had cowboy boots, but one day Walt Jenson discarded a worn and very muddy pair he'd grown tired of. Even though they were too big, I commandeered them, cleaned them up, polished them until they shone, and that fall took them to college for special occasions. There I found that girls liked cowboys.

The summer I spent earning a dollar per day on the 7-11 ranch provided me with two things that were to serve me well in the future: I learned there are better ways to earn a living than being a cowboy, which motivated me for a successful college career, and when I wore those boots, they provided me with a great "line" for use with the college girls -- "Yes, I was once a cowboy."

Bill and me -- two tough hombres. The house on the left was the O'Bannon house, where we lived for a few years, then later in the Sprague house, which is behind the photographer. On the right you can see a portion of the Sewright horse corrals and barn.

Yes, I am still a cowboy on my 3 acre ranch near Sonora, where I raise herds of marauding deer and stray cats.

THIRTEEN: A FOOTBALL AFTERNOON

We're loyal to you Edgemont Hi.
We're loyal to you Edgemont Hi.
We'll back you to stand,
You're the best in the land
For we know you've got stand
Edgemont Hi, RAH, RAH, RAH.

My high school fight song went something like that, but I never knew it well, because I was not in the pep squad; I was always out on the football field getting the tar kicked out of me. I loved to play football, but to be honest; I liked touch football better. Today I would love to play soccer even more, except during my youth it had not yet made it across the Atlantic Ocean.

Football is physically challenging and was even more so in the 1940s when I played in high school. In Edgemont you played the entire game, because our school was so small we had few substitutes. Also, the rules were different back then; you played both ways: offense and defense. If you were substituted and came out of the game, you could not enter again for that entire half.

I was the team quarterback on offense and the team safety on defense. Since there was no backup quarterback, if I was injured and had to leave the game, a halfback would shift to quarterback and the end to halfback. It wasn't good for the flow of the game. Whenever I got the wind knocked out of me and lay prone on the field, the coach would come out with a bottle of smelling salts to hold under my nose until I was able to regain my feet and stay in the game. Against the Custer High School team, that happened three times to me in one game.

It was fun to play on the Hot Springs football field because it was grass and therefore soft. You hit the ground like falling on a mattress when you got tackled. Not so on our Edgemont field, which was hard dirt. One year the Custer team threatened to forfeit rather than play there. Our football field was on the rodeo grounds directly in front of the bucking shoots. That year it had rained on rodeo day, and all the bronco hoof ruts dried and became like razor-sharp corrugated. When you saw a tackler coming at you, you'd look for a rut-free place to land before submitting to the tackle. I swear that is the truth.

In 1945, Edgemont had its best winning team in a decade. During the traditional Armistice Day game against Hot Springs, I was knocked unconscious in the fourth quarter, but regained my feet with smelling salts. I stayed in the game, called the plays, and we won. It was not until after the game in the shower room that teammates and the coach realized I was out of my head. I kept asking over and over, "who won?" "We did?" and I'd cheer again and again. The coach took me home where my parents placed me in bed. I remained there for a week before I returned to normal. Teammates tell me it was a highlight of my football career, but to this day I remember nothing of the game.

It is hard to explain why boys play football. I cannot explain it even today, except perhaps from peer pressure. However, there is a strong bond among a team. It has been sixty-five years since I played on my high school team, but I can still name every player and his position on our winning 1945 team:

QBBernie Keating

LHArt Pearse

FBJoe Daum

RHHerman Boner

LEGene Parks

LTRaymond Barkley

LG John Gallegos

CFred Guynn

RGChub Bergen

RTEarle Boner

RE Bob Claphan.

Today, there are only three of us still alive. When we get together, we always re-tell our story of beating Hot Springs in the big Armistice Day game. Being on the team seemed to define a high point in our young lives. It identified us as macho men.

Yes, I loved it. Would I do it again? It is difficult to make those kinds of decisions in hindsight. Probably. High school football provided me with a life-long discipline, competitive instinct, ability to ignore minor pain, loyalty to a team, and above all, a reason to excel. Yes, I'm sure, I would do it again.

The quarterback #36, still my lucky number

This is the 1946 team when I was a senior. We lost most our starters from the previous year of 1945, when we won all but one game, so this team learned how to lose with pride.

FOURTEEN: THE SWEETHEART OF SIGMA CHI

The girl of my dreams is the sweetest girl of all the girls I know;
Each sweet co-ed, like a rainbow trail, fades in the afterglow.
The blue of her eyes and the gold of her hair, are a blend of the western sky; and the moonlight beams on the girl of my dreams, She's the sweetheart of Sigma Chi. [7]

This fraternity song, more than any other, symbolizes college romance, and it has always been a favorite of mine, even though I was not a Sigma Chi. I wasn't even much of a ladies' man in college; I was too damn shy. But I do love that song; a guy can fantasy, can't he? When my older brother, Edwin, and I arrived at the University of Colorado campus in the fall of 1947, I did not even know what a fraternity was. We had none in Buffalo Gap. As I wandered up University Avenue, I wondered what those Greek symbols over the doorways of some fancy houses meant.

Edwin and I shared one room in a boarding house on the north side of Boulder, the opposite end of town from the campus. It was a three mile walk each way, lugging our books, and that got old very fast. The room was the only place available, because the war had just ended and the university was overrun with ex-GI's returning to college.

During the war years, virtually all the fraternities had become inactive, because there were so few males on campus; but several were now recruiting to become active again. One day, we saw the announcement of a meeting to reactive the Delta Sigma Phi fraternity, and their house was located across the street from the campus entrance. What an ideal location. We went to the meeting, and my brother was suddenly elected president of the fraternity. Hooray! Now we had a room in the fraternity house, which saved a six mile walk every day. We were also in the center of campus life. Talk about farm boys moving from Timbuktu to the Big Apple! We became typical fraternity jocks, and Edwin even started dating sorority girls. It took a while before I did; I was so damn shy.

The University in Boulder has always been known as a "party" school. If it was, I am one guy who never made it to the party. I was carrying 18 hours of engineering courses plus another 3 hours of navy subjects, because I was on a NROTC scholarship. Don't get me wrong; I'm not complaining, because the navy was paying for my tuition and fees, bought all my books and engineering instruments, paid me $50 per month, and supplied me with uniforms, which I often wore to class to save on clothing costs. Without all that government income, college was not an option for me, or certainly not at a top-notch university. I was poor as a church mouse, but scrapped by with few luxuries. I waited tables my freshman year in the fraternity house, and starting in my sophomore year I cooked breakfast with the help of two other guys. I was a good cook, and served breakfast for the fraternity crew of twenty five guys. The kitchen jobs supplied my pocket change for college. The breakfasts I cooked consisted of fried eggs, buttered toast with jelly, pancakes or French toast with honey or syrup, fried potatoes, and coffee; and still I finished in time to make it to my 8:00 am chemistry class. I never got any complaints from my cooking. That indicated the value of my cuisine experience from Buffalo Gap.

Since I made good grades during my first two years, I was elected to a scholarship honorary. Unfortunately, when I became an upperclassman and went to a counselor to help me decide which branch of engineering to pursue, he steered me down a tough path. He considered my IQ test results of 135 and convinced me I should go into engineering physics; he did not tell me it was probably the toughest major in college. I was to find that out when I hit those upperclassmen advanced math and physics classes. I was barely hanging on academically.

Delta Sigma Phi fraternity was not one of the high status social clubs at Boulder; that honor went to fraternities such as Sigma Alpha Epsilon, Sigma Chi, or Sigma Nu. The famous bandleader, Glenn Miller was a Sigma Nu when he attended the University. Of the twenty fraternities and twenty sororities on campus, mine was probably ranked socially by the sorority girls in the bottom third. Kappa Kappa Gamma and Alpha Phi sorority girls were always hoping for a date with a guy from Sigma Alpha Epsilon. Over half my fraternity brothers were mature ex-GIs who did attract the ladies. Bob Morgan had been a B-24 bomber pilot and Keith Sanders was a bombardier; they never lacked for dates.

I had trouble to find the courage to feed a line to some girl and then ask her for a date, particularly if she was a sorority girl. I dated very little in high school, plus I had virtually no time for serious dating in college. I obtained a used tux that I wore to fraternity and sorority formals, usually with a blind date that someone fixed me up with. Romancing a girl took experience, money, and a lot of time and energy -- a real commitment. Instead, I spent most my evenings and weekends in the library with my head in a physics book, not by choice but for survival.

Don't get me wrong; I loved college life, and looking back, it was one of the most fun times of my life. There is no more exciting experience than a Saturday football afternoon on the Boulder campus, particularly if you have a date with a cute blond sorority girl to take to the game and to the homecoming dance afterwards. Those dates didn't happen often with me, but in my dreams, I can fantasy.

I liked my experience with the NROTC naval unit and did very well. In my senior year I was appointed company commander and I had to wear a sword with my uniform. That meant that on Thursday afternoon which was drill day, I had to wear my full uniform and carry a sword to all my classes. Carrying a sword around campus was embarrassing, and it never fit well hanging from my side in a classroom desk. At graduation I was ranked second in the naval unit and that would have meant considerable later in my career if I had decided to stay in the navy. I was commissioned an Ensign USN on graduation day and immediately was assigned to a destroyer off the Korean coast in shore bombardment. In May I was a fraternity guy in college, and a month later I was picking targets to blast in North Korea. After three combat tours, I decided a navy career was not for me; I got out.

College was not yet over for me. I went to graduate school at the University of California, Berkeley. The GI Bill was helpful but I needed more resources, so I became a teaching assistant in the Engineering Department, and joined the active naval reserve at Treasure Island one night each week for which I got full days pay as a Lieutenant J.G. Now I had my own apartment, a car, some money, more free time, and I loved it. Then I got a job and started a career.

After six years of college and several college degrees, what had I learned? That is difficult to appraise. The two courses that probably helped me most during my career were psychology and public speaking. Then later in night school I took creative writing and that would also rank in the top three. During my career I went almost immediately into management jobs, so never did work directly in engineering. It is hard to say how much my engineering discipline helped me. Probably the most valuable experience from my college years was learning how to work hard and persevere.

And the moon light beams on the girl of my dreams
She's the sweetheart of Sigma Chi

My Sweetheart, Aurdery, when she was a little girl.
We were married on May 3rd, 1958, on the day of the Kentucky Derby. Every time I hear the Derby will be run on Saturday, I know it is time for me to purchase a box of chocolates as a gift to my lady. I must confess, I also take her out to dinner to celebrate that wonderful event of over fifty years ago when she became my bride.

My sister, Betty, when she was in college. On graduation day, she married Frank Stanko, who was the star of the football team at Colorado College.

Betty was one year younger than I, and during all the years in Buffalo Gap, she was my best friend. We were hiking buddies, and on Saturdays we climbed through all the canyons west of town

Aurdery and I met during a moonlight cruise to the Corinthian Yacht Club in the spring of 1957. I saw her across the dance floor, and thought, WOW!!

I invited her to join me for a coffee, but she ordered a full hamburger dinner instead. In December when Aurdery joined two roommates for a skiing vacation at Timberline Lodge in Oregon, I invited myself along. I proposed at midnight on New Year's Eve, and the rest is history.

Then a month later, I went home to Fresno with Aurdery to meet her parents. If I look nervous, that's why. At that point Aurdery and her mother took over all the wedding arrangements, and we were married on May 3rd, 1958, in Saint Theresa Catholic Church with a huge reception to follow under a tent that covered her parent's entire yard.

Our honeymoon was at the Miramar Resort in Santa Barbara, and then a visit to Hollywood.

FIFTEEN: *I'LL BE HOME FOR CHRISTMAS*

... Christmas Eve will find me
Where the love light beams.
I'll be home for Christmas,
If only in my dreams. [8]

... and one year it was only in my dreams. The song carries me back to Christmas Eve in 1951 when I was in combat and a long way from home.

My ship was in the enemy port, Wonson, North Korea, where we circled day and night with our five inch guns blasting salvos against the shore on all sides. My destroyer had been inside the harbor now for two weeks with a trip every third day outside to the ammunition ship and replenish our supply of projectiles. The roads and railroads of the enemy were forced down to this port by the high mountains of the interior; so we harassed them endlessly. Our job was to create havoc. Our destroyer, the USS Boyd, circled from one end of the harbor to the other, guns blasting. With air cover support from above, we could not be driven out.

My combat post was in the fire control station high above the bridge where I picked the targets for our five inch batteries and pulled the trigger. Eight hours on, four hours off, round the clock, wearing side arms, helmet, life jacket, and foul weather jacket -- it was freezing cold. The ship got little incoming fire because the enemy's shore batteries had been destroyed, but we feared the floating mines which could sink a ship in minutes. Three minesweepers worked day and night to clear them away. In the darkness of night, the enemy sent small boats to launch these lethal floating weapons. Hitting one meant a quick trip to the bottom. Two ships had already gone to that grave, with most men carried down with their ship. What would the last moments be like for those caught inside the water graveyard?

From 4 pm to midnight on Christmas Eve, I picked the targets and pulled the trigger. Then at midnight after I headed below, I paused for a moment to think of home and my father and mother. They would go to midnight Mass, then home for eggnog by the Christmas tree, and there would be turkey tomorrow. That brief moment dreaming of home was my Christmas.

I survived that horrible time, and now many years later, I am with my own family beside a Christmas tree. But every time I hear that song, I pause and think of all those other men and women still on duty around the world, dreaming of home.

Tomorrow is Christmas, and I must arise early to get the turkey in the oven. I know the procedure well. Set the oven at 325 F degree, remove the neck and giblets from the body cavity, rinse the bird with cold water, rub the body and cavity with salt, and stuff the bird. Then rub the entire turkey with a paste made of the following:

4 Tablespoons of saffola oil.

4 Teaspoons salt.

2 Teaspoons paprika.

Place the bird in the oven breast side up and add two 8 oz glasses of water. When the turkey is half done, lightly heat one cup of white wine and pour over the turkey, which is a great addition for the gravy.

A twenty pound hen will take 15 minutes per pound, or 5 hours. Press a meat thermometer into the thigh and be careful not to over-roast, because no one likes dry turkey. There is no need to turn the bird while roasting as it will brown to a rich, golden color; however, a piece of foil should be placed loosely over the turkey approximately the last hour of roasting.

Now for the gravy. Throw away the liver and place the giblets and neck in a pan of water with onions, carrots, parsley, three bulbs of garlic, two chicken bouillon cubes and one beef bouillon cube, and bring to a boil for a half hour. Drain through a colander, catching the fluid which will be a base for the gravy. Cut up the vegetables and giblets, pull the meat off the neck, and add to the liquid. Pour the droppings from the bottom of the roasting pan into a tall glass jar which is cooled so the grease rises to the top and can be skimmed off. The brown droppings on the bottom of the jar are a great addition to the gravy.

Place a small portion of this fluid into a frying pan, stirring in several tablespoons of gravy flour to form a thick paste, and gradually add the rest of the fluid. Add some milk or cream. Gravy must be cooked slowly and stirred to avoid scorching. Occasionally sample the flavor and adjust seasoning. The cook is entitled to an occasional sip of chardonnay wine, and adds a half cup to the gravy.

It is usually the man of the house who is asked to carve the turkey, but many are intimidated by the prospect of the job. Perhaps this is because they watched an old movie with Lionel Barrymore carving at the dining room table. God forbid -- that's Hollywood. Carving should be done in the kitchen. Forty years ago, I gave an electric carving knife to my father-in-law; but he refused to use it, preferring his old butcher knife. So he returned it to me and it still works perfectly once each year to carve the Christmas turkey.

Almost anyone can roast a turkey, but the measure of a good cook is the gravy. A gravy "to die for" tops off a wonderful dinner.

...

> *`I'll be home for Christmas.*
> *If only in my dreams.*

This year I am home for Christmas ... and Christmas Eve finds me where the love light beams. The best time of the year is Christmas Eve with family and friends, and a Christmas dinner with roast turkey and sumptuous gravy?

Aurdery and I on our wedding day. Isn't she gorgeous?

Aurdery and I at home with all our family on Christmas Day in 2007

SIXTEEN: VENISON ALA KEATING

Old King Cole was a merry old soul
And a merry old soul was he.
He called for his pipe, and he called for his bowl
And he called for his fiddlers three.
Every fiddler he had a fiddle,
And a very fine fiddle had he,
Oh there's none so rare, as can compare
With King Cole and his fiddlers three.

The historical identity of this nursery rhyme has been much debated, but it first appeared in written form over three hundred years ago in 1708, and its origin goes back much earlier. A king named Coel ruled in the northern part of England. He was a Roman commander who turned his command into a kingdom as the Roman Empire crumbled and declared himself King. There are several other accounts to explain the legend, so anyone is free to make their own. Here is George Carlin's version (he was allegedly a drug user).

Old King Cole was a merry old soul
And a merry old soul was he.
He called for his pipe and he called for his bowl --
I guess we all know about Old King Cole.

Altered lyrics have been used in comic books, TV shows, Video games, and film. Walt Disney made the cartoon, *Silly Symphony*, in 1933 called *Old King Cole* in which the King holds a huge party where various nursery rhyme characters are invited.

None of the legends for Old King Cole are traced back to King Henry VIII, the English guy with all those wives. Too bad, because that would have provided me with a segue to talk about his recipe for venison. It is the earliest written English recipe I have found. (See Chapter Twenty Six, Mediterranean Cuisine, which gives the earliest recipes of the Greeks.) I doubt that King Henry spent much time in the kitchen, but I found his chef's venison recipe, which was his favorite meal. While King Henry was no cook, apparently he did occasionally kill his own deer in the game preserves maintained near his Windsor Castle.

Like Henry, I also come from a hunting family. When my father was a boy living at the Cuyhoga Gold Mining Camp in the Black Hills with his father, he was a hillbilly who hunted to provide meals for his father and younger brother. As an adult after he became a banker, Dad's hobby was hunting, and from earliest days it was also in my blood. The opening day of hunting season in South Dakota was November 1st; that day always found us in the woods stalking deer with a 30-30 carbine in our hands. While we hunted for sport, we also were motivated to put meat on the table: rabbit, pheasant, duck, geese, elk, and venison.

Since I retired in recent years, I again have started to hunt in the Sierra Mountains near where I live. During the last dozen years, I have bagged only two deer, so venison feeds are few and far between. However, I have found leg of lamb to be a reasonable substitute. I recently looked up venison on the internet and found a listing for a couple deer farms in the United States where it can be purchased, and that is a good avenue to pursue. I plan to get some and have a venison dinner next year.

Now to King Henry's recipe. Start by placing the meat in the following marinate:

Red wine, enough to cover the meat.

Half a dozen bulbs of pressed garlic

Four peppercorns plus some ground pepper

2 tablespoons of tarragon, plus some bay leaf.

Just before cooking, remove the meat and save ½ cup of marinate for a sauce.

Now, let's address the vegetables for the feast, and remember this meal is prepared by macho male deer hunters. You could assign vegetable preparation to the housewife; however, this is not recommended because the vegetable must convey a rugged, masculine appearance, which means they must be el dente -- undercooked -- whereas most housewives tend to over-cook vegetables. Also, two cooks in one kitchen present well-known problems.

Sauté several huge mushrooms in butter into which fresh garlic bulbs have been pressed. Remove when under-cooked and place in the warming oven, saving the garlic butter. Cook small red potatoes in the microwave, removing when under-cooked and still crunchy, swish around in the garlic butter, and set aside in the warming oven. Do the same with small carrots, and now turn your attention to preparation of the sauce which will be poured over the meat. While preparation of the sauce seems complicated, remember this is a ceremonial occasion, so take your time and enjoy.

1. Melt two beef bouillon cubes in ¼ cup of hot water.
2. In a skillet, dice eight strips of salt pork and cook until the dices are rendered. Pour off the grease and save the residue from the bottom.

3. Into the above skillet pour the bouillon, the butter-garlic, and ½ cup of marinate, and stir in two tablespoons of flour.

4. Now come the best part, and it becomes apparent why delegation should be avoided. Open a bottle of apricot brandy. Taste some to insure it has proper flavor, and pour ½ cup into the sauce. If guests are in the kitchen, and have been laudatory, offer them a sample.

5. Set the skillet off the heat so it does not burn.

6. The final step in the sauce preparation (and do this just before serving) is to add one cup of sour cream, stir, reheat, and taste. Add more brandy if necessary. This sauce should be poured over the meat just prior to serving.

Now for the *piece' a da resistance*:

1. Preheat the oven to 450F.

2. Use a glass casserole dish.

3. On top of each piece of meat place a thin strip of salt pork. The strip will be discarded when done.

4. Place the meat in the oven. Use an oven thermometer.

5. Depending on the thickness of the roast, it is often done in 15 minutes or less. It is best served when medium with some pinkness in the center.

So the spouse will have a sense of participation, let her prepare the salad, dessert, set the table, do the dishes afterwards, and other unskilled activities. You are the macho artisan skilled for this particular meal.

Let the feast begin. Remember this is more than just a meal, it is a semi-religious tradition that starts in the woods, moves into the kitchen and then to the dining room. A bottle of pinot noir will go nicely. The host should offer a toast to the health of his guests, and then raise his glass for a second toast:

"A toast to the recipe of King Henry VIII, may he rest in Hell, where I 'm sure he is, and may we never have occasion to visit him there. Salute."

The Englhardt family joins us for a Christmas Eve dinner of my King VIII venison. Aurdery is the photographer behind the camera. From the left are Lorie, Zachary, Deke, Me, Carson, Eric, McKenna, and Addison. We have venison so seldom; it is too early to call it a Christmas Eve tradition. The last time was a dozen years ago at my daughter's, Treci Dimas, in New York. Next year we will order a venison roast from a deer farm in Kansas, so it may become a tradition in the future.

Lorie and Eric Wedding in November 1997. They were married in St Patrick church, Sonora, with Father Kraft presiding. The reception was held in the Sonora OperaHall, and it was the reception held there after its renovation that year. Front row are Angela and Ari Dimas. Back row are George and Treci Dimas, me, the wedding couple, mother of the bride, Roger and Deke.

SEVENTEEN: DAD'S FRIDAY NIGHT CIOPPINO

I don't know if my recipe should be called bouillabaisse, which came to us from the French port of Marseille; or called cioppino, which is what it was named at Calibrini's little shop on a side street near my factory in Oakland, when I stopped on Friday nights on the way home to pick up a quart jar; or called fish stew, which was on the menu at the Sea Wolf restaurant in Jack London Square on the Oakland estuary; or called cacciucco, which is an Italian fish stew which originated in the Mediterranean port of Livorno; but whichever name it goes by, it has always been a favorite Friday night dish with my family. When I started to make it with my improvised recipe many years ago, it became an instant hit and has always been referred to as "Dad's Friday Night Cioppino."

That little shop in Oakland has not existed now for four decades -- since Calibrini died -- and perhaps its demise may be as a result of questionable activities. I suspected some of the warehouse workers were "liberating" cartons of empty glass jars from my factory warehouse and providing them to Calibrini, in return for his "gratis" Friday night jars of cioppino to take home.

His shop was on a side street two blocks west of the Fruitvale Bridge where the factory was located. You couldn't miss the glass factory with the five brick smokestacks that rose 200 feet into the air. To reach his shop, circle around behind the Del Monte catsup plant and go down the dead-end alley toward the estuary. It was so out-of-the-way that it is surprising anyone ever found it, and I don't know how I first heard of it; probably from one of my warehousemen? I was always especially popular with them for some reason. Perhaps it had less to do with me than them spending their days in isolation in the endless aisles of the huge warehouse, pallets stacked four high twenty feet into the air, and I was one of the few people they ever saw. That was because I enjoyed my solitary walks through warehouse aisles during the lunch-hour break. As they rode their high lifts down the aisle, we always shared a hello, and often a few minutes to pass the latest news or joke.

The quiet walk in the warehouse was in contrast to the atmosphere in my hectic office located in the middle of the factory, surrounded by a thousand people who worked round the clock on twenty six production lines, twenty-four hours per day and seven days, manufacturing and packaging three million bottle each day. My day started at 5am when I climbed out of bed, then the half-hour commute to the factory, and I was usually met at my office door by either a union officer or one of my supervisors with the crisis of the moment. If possible, I quickly escaped for a one-hour observation walk through the hot-end where glass was melted in five furnaces and bottles were manufactured on twenty six machines along a two hundred foot production line; then through the cold end where three million bottles passed down conveyors to be packed into corrugated boxes; and then into the palletizing area where conveyors delivered filled boxes to be stacked onto pallets, and carried into the warehouse by high lift.

The first meeting began at 7:15 am in my office, and it was a short, stand-up meeting with supervisors and foreman to assess the early priorities for the day. Then began a day of this and that, identifying problems, solving un-solvable problems with the least worse solution, meetings with the union, more meetings with others, getting chewed out by a Sales Manager for the poor quality delivered to his customer, a short discussion with the personnel director, a joke with a foreman, a hello to some workers in the corrugated department, a quiet moment with the office door closed for a breather and a look at the mail, and a brown bag sandwich and diet Coke for lunch. Then to the warehouse aisles for my solitary walk.

After a long afternoon with more of the same, I walked to my car at 5:30 and waved to the guard as I exited the plant. I was well paid as a manager, but it was a tough job, and I was emotionally drained at the end of the day. This being Friday night, I circled around behind the Del Monte catsup plant and headed down the alley to Calibrini's for a jar of cioppino, a loaf of sourdough bread, and a bottle of wine to take home. The family would be waiting for me.

Then Calibrini died, and there was no more cioppino to take home. What to do? The answer, of course, was to make my own.

While cioppino may have been originated with the memory of the Italian dish, cacciucco, which immigrants carried to this country, it was developed in the late 1800s by Italian fishermen who settled in the North Beach section of San Francisco. Originally cioppino was made on the fishing boats while out at sea and later became a staple as Italian restaurants proliferated in San Francisco. The name comes from Ciuppin, a word in the Ligurian dialect of the port city of Genoa, meaning "to chop" or "chopped", which described the process of making the stew by chopping up various leftovers of the days catch.

Acting on the description provided me by the chef at one of the restaurants on Fisherman's Wharf; I decided to invent my own creation. After all, if fishermen could make it on a rocking boat at sea with limited resources, I should be able to do it in my kitchen. You will find my recipe very simple and easy to prepare, so don't begin to over-complicate it. As the Friday nights pass by, you can add your own cuisine embellishments in future weeks.

For a family of six, start with a very large pot. Throw in 1 cup of canola oil (olive oil if you prefer). Chop 2 large onions and place in the simmering oil to sauté. Add a half cup of water. Then throw into the pot the following:

8-10 cloves of garlic

6 bay leaves

2 bunches of chopped fresh parsley

1 14oz can of chicken broth

2 small cans of clam juice

3 cubes of beef bouillon

1 tablespoon of oregano (or Italian seasoning)

2 tablespoons of sugar

Salt and pepper

2 or 3 chopped carrots

2 diced potatoes

1 chopped bell pepper

1 6oz can of tomato paste (I formerly used 2 cans, but now prefer less tomato taste and have added the chicken broth

Simmer the above for 20 minutes.

Now comes the fish, and I use what is available fresh, but will not hesitate to use frozen filets of a white fish. (The famous Scoma's restaurant on fisherman's Wharf uses only clams, crab, and prawns in their cioppino. They also don't use carrots or diced potato, but I like my creation better.)

Unless fresh sea bass or cod is available, I would probably use several filets of a frozen white fish. Cut it into bite size pieces and throw in the pot. When fresh clams are available, I throw a dozen in the pot. Mussels can be used instead. I lightly crack a dozen crab legs and throw them in the pot, shells and all. Remove the shells from 2 dozen uncooked shrimp and throw in the pot. Cover and continue to simmer until the fish is just cooked through, about 15-25 minutes. Do not overcook.

If you happen to be French and more refined than my Italian family, and you want bouillabaisse instead of cioppino; no problem. Remove the shells from the shell fish before throwing them in the pot. The flavor is little changed, but absent the shells, the meal does lose something of the tradition; particularly with the children, who have never seen such things in their dish before.

Now occurs a most important ingredient, especially if it is Friday night. Open a bottle of chardonnay wine and add 2 cups to the pot. To insure it is a good wine, pour some goblets for you and your spouse, and do some sampling. (Some people prefer a red wine in cioppino, but I think a white enhances the fish creation better.)

As you sip the wine, do some tasting of the pot. Add whatever seasoning needs enhancement. I suspect it will need more Italian seasoning. Perhaps you will want more tomato paste. Sampling can be messy, so tear off a hunk of sourdough bread and use as a coaster to catch the drips.

When the family sits down to the meal, bow your heads for a short prayer in thanksgiving for a great week and a fine meal. Friday nights never get better than cioppino and all the family together around the table.

My Mother and Dad on a great time in the 1960's when they joined Aurdery and me for a day of salmon fishing on a small sport boat out of Depot Bat, The occasion fulfilled a life-long dream for my Dad, who had always looked forward to such a day.

EIGHTEEN:USS BOYD DD544

TENDERLY [9]

... The shore was kissed by sea and mist tenderly
I can't forget how two hearts met breathlessly
Your arms opened wide and closed me inside
You took my lips, you took my love so tenderly.

Let me set the stage. It is 1951; I am on a destroyer, the USS Boyd
DD544; we are in Task Force 77 off the coast of Korea where the
aircraft carrier is launching planes against North Korea, I am off-duty
for a couple hours drinking coffee in the officers' wardroom, alone,
except for two afro-American stewards who stand nearby in event I ask
for anything, and on the stereo in the corner Sarah Vaughan is singing
"Tenderly" to me. Except, perhaps, not singing to me, but to the two
mess stewards who bought the recording.

This is my first combat tour in Korean Waters (I was to see two more
years of combat) and I am alone, a long way from home, and lonely.
Sarah seems to be singing only to me, and I am hearing every word:
"Then you and I came wandering by and lost in a sigh were we."

The wardroom is bouncing as the ship goes to flank speed at 35
knots, heading to the port stern of the aircraft carrier, which is about
to launch aircraft. Our ship is on lifeguard duty close behind the carrier

in a position to recover any pilots whose planes ditch into the water on takeoff. The carrier will speed on, but we will stop suddenly, launch a lifeboat, and recover the swimming pilot if he made it out of the sinking plane. Sometime they did and then we'd pass the pilot back to the carrier by bosom chair -- a canvas chair hanging on ropes that swung him over to the carrier. We'd get a message of thanks from the carrier, and often the gift of a crate of fresh fruit. Other times the pilot did not make it; he went down with his plane, and the radio would remain silent.

When the seas were rough and we were at 35 knots, riding the destroyer was a challenge. Waves crashed over the bow as we heaved into them, sending spray over the bridge. If I were in my stateroom below, I would be laying on my bunk because it was too unstable to sit in my chair at the desk. I wrote letters home to my parents when the seas were smooth and we were cruising at 18 knots; so my penmanship conveyed an image of tranquility.

I had been trained for this life aboard ship. Four years as a Midshipman in college and three summers of NROTC cruises had prepared me well for being a naval officer. Life at sea was what it was all about. Now here I was: life at sea, combat, war, loneliness, seeing death up close, return to port, liberty in Japan, bar hopping in Black Market Alley, and then back to sea again with more combat. Next assignment was shore bombardment of the North Korean port, Wonson.

The wardroom was where we ate and also where we spent our time with other officers when not on duty or below in our stateroom. We always had good music on the stereo. The records were not purchased by us officers, nor supplied by the U.S. Navy. No. They were the compliments of the Afro-American mess stewards who grew tired of silence and wanted to hear music to liven up their days. With their own money, they purchased the recordings-of-the-day, which were usually Sarah Vaughan, Billy Eckstine, or Rosemary Clooney. Sarah would sing her song, *Misty:* *"Look at me, I am helpless as a kitten up a tree; and I feel like I'm clinging to a cloud, I can't understand. I get misty, just holding your hand."* And then sing her Grammy-winning song: *Tenderly:* *"You took my lips, you took my love, so tenderly."*

After thirty days, we pulled alongside an oiler to be refueled and sacks of mail were delivered by rope over to our ship. It was mail call. My letters were mostly from my parents and often a package of cookies. I lived for those messages from home, and hearing what was going on back there. After three years at sea, my letters must have been dull, always the same old things about shipboard life. What's new this week? Nothing; more sailing.

Sailors in the mess hall get food supplied free by the U.S. Navy, but it different for officers. Our monthly pay included an allowance for food, so we were expected to pay for our meals, even at sea when though all the food came from the ship's holds below. One officer is elected as the "Wardroom Officer". He had two responsibilities: one was to "consult" with the head mess steward and decide on menus, and the second was to collect from each officer his monthly allowance to pay for meals. It is an elective office, and guess who is usually elected? You guessed it: the newest ensign aboard ship. After I arrived aboard by bosom chair swung over from a tanker alongside and still shaking from the harrowing experience, I was greeted on deck by the Executive Officer, taken to the bridge to meet the Captain, shown the cramped stateroom I would share with five other ensigns, and then congratulated on being elected the new Wardroom Officer.

Wardroom officer: what the hell did that mean? The first thing that came with the assignment was listening to the gripes of all the officers about the menu and my lack of interesting dishes -- all of which came out of the ship's hold below. The second subject included their gripes about my monthly bill for their meals (which was always identical to the food allowance they were receiving). Then a third subject was to remind me they expected a great lobster feed after four weeks at sea when we finally got back to port in Sasebo, Japan. Lobster? I had never seen a lobster, yet alone eat one -- or serve a great meal of them.

After a month at sea, we finally came to port, and you could smell it when approaching from two miles out. Perhaps coming from the fresh air at sea, all ports smell somewhat, but none more than Japanese ports in the aftermath of World War II after their entire infrastructure had been destroyed and no sewer facilities remained. Human defecate flowed down open ditches alongside the streets. It took two days and two nights of heavy drinking in local bars to get acclimated to the smell.

The other officers went ashore, but I was still aboard to meet with the head mess steward and make plans for a lobster dinner. He knew the ropes, and had already contacted a lobster boat and made the arrangements. "Mister Keating, your thirty lobsters are delivered, sir, and they are up on the fo 'sol deck."

I went forward and saw thirty live lobsters crawling on the deck. I told him, "Chief, take over."

He responded, "Yes sir, we will have that great lobster feed tonight." I do not know what he did, but I assume he got boiling water, threw the lobsters in a pot, and that night I became a hero to the officers aboard ship. The only thing that would have made it better was a goblet of chardonnay wine, but of course, all alcohol is forbidden aboard a U.S. Navy ship.

I remained Wardroom Officer for another two months at sea until the next ensign came aboard. As soon as he got out of the canvas bosom chair, I rushed up and congratulated him on his election as the new Wardroom Officer.

War is hell.

Dick (Buck) Rogers and I are the last two living officers (that we know of) who served together sixty years ago on the USS Boyd DD 544. We were good friends aboard ship where we shared the 6 person junior officer stateroom, nicknamed the "arm Pit", and we did many of our liberties together. Buck retired as a Captain, USN, after a long career as a naval legal officer. We still get together each year at his home in Virginia Beach.

NINETEEN: COQUILLE ST.
JACQUES AU GRATIN

In the 1958 Parisian film, *Gigi*, Maurice Chevalier sang the delightful song, *I Remember It Well*, with Hermione Gingold who chides him for his lapses of memory. He does the remembering, and Hermione corrects him **in bold print** and with a bold voice.

The lyrics have special meaning to me since I am often admonished by my wife of fifty two years for my fading memory of things when I was courting her.

I REMEMBER IT WELL [10]

*We met at nine, **we met at eight**, I was on time, **no,***
You were late
Ah, yes, I remember it well
*We dined with friends, **we dined alone,***
*a tenor sang, **a baritone***
Ah, yes, I remember it well

*That dazzling April moon, **there was none that night***
*And the month was June, **that's right, that's right***
It warms my heart to know that you

Remember still the way you do
Ah, yes, I remember it well

... You were a crown of gold,
It was all in blue
Am I getting old? **Oh, no, not you**
How strong you were, how young and gay
A prince of love in every way
Ah, yes, I remember it well

I have visited France many times, first in my role as a consultant to my company's glass making French affiliate, BSN, and more recently when my wife and I were tourists.

I love France, the French people, and French cuisine. If they are stand-offish and unfriendly as some have said, I certainly did not experience it. Of course during my initial encounter I was treated very well because I had something to provide -- my expertise. As the Corporate Manager of Quality Assurance for Owens Illinois, the world's leading glassmaker, I had responsibilities for the quality in 25 factories and 35 sales branches in the United States and for providing quality leadership to our oversea affiliates in 33 countries around the world; hence, I knew my way around a glass factory. This provided me with international credibility, and I was treated well as I travelled to our oversea affiliates. They were paying big money to my company for my services, and they expected results in helping them with their problems. I was expected to have the answers and provide solutions to tough problems. That brings me to France where I spent time in half a dozen of their factories.

While our French affiliate was interested in my expertise in the quality area, I often found they needed me more as a hatchet man from out-of-town to help them discharge huge chunks of their labor force that existed because of featherbedding. Of the dozens of countries I have assisted around the world, France had the most troublesome labor force, because of arcane national laws and unfair union work rules.

In a Northern factory near Cambria, I assisted them in discharging 80 unneeded workers. Another factory in Reims, which produced virtually all the Champagne bottles in France, was operating in the red and in danger of being abandoned. After extensive study, I decided they had 150 more workers than needed. The workforce was intentionally producing some defective product to provide jobs for dozens of family members who worked in rework departments sorting and culling out the defects. The plant management had the challenge of how to tackle this cost and labor problem without jeopardizing the quality of their finished product. It was the same kind of problem I had faced many previous times in my management career, and there was never an easy answer. I made my recommendation for the workforce reduction, which they immediately executed, and as I exited the plant, pickets appeared to begin a 60 day strike.

One year later I was invited back and hailed as a hero, at least by the management and those workers who had jobs and were still on the payroll. The plant had survived and did not shut down. It was now operating profitably in the black, and remained the top quality supplier of glass containers to the champagne industry. I was received warmly, even by the hourly workforce, because they felt I had saved the plant and their jobs.

I knew in advance of this success; so I asked my wife to accompany me on the return trip. Reims is the jewel of France. While I was working ten hour days climbing among the furnaces and conveyors of the glass factory, my wife was hosted by the plant manager's wife and guided through the beautiful city, which includes one of the world's most historic cathedrals and also the World War II headquarters of General Eisenhower. She also got a guided tour through the champagne cellars, something I was not able to accomplish until a dozen years later when I was a tourist.

In a highlight of that trip, we were hosted to a dinner with the glass factory management group in one of the most beautiful restaurants in Europe, which featured floral settings enhanced by exotic birds. That experience was our introduction to Coquille St. Jacques. I have eaten food all over the world, and each culture excels with their native dishes. However, I think French cuisine is the best. I am not talking about the restaurants of Paris that specialize in dishes for tourist with a lot of sauces, but rather the simple French food found in the provinces where the glass factories were usually located. The food there is very simple, vegetables are cooked "el dente", each course is served on specialized dinnerware, and dinner is accompanied with an unhurried conversation. While I was normally provided with an interpreter, I found most educated French spoke some English, and I occasionally accommodated them with a bit of my fractured French.

I had similar experiences in other oversea factories where I provided technical expertise with their problems. Here are a few snapshots from my travels:

In another factory in Northern France, I found vending machines providing 187 ml. liters of wine available to the work force. By mid-shift most of them were so snookered they could not tell a bottle from a tin can.

In Italy where I visited 8 of their factories, I had been called in as a referee between the manufacturing group and the sales force. The factory people felt sales did not know how to sell their excellent product, and the sales force said their customers were being shipped a pile of junk. The Italians never accepted any of my recommendations, but they loved me and invited me back three years in a row. I finally realized my recommendations were "dead on arrival". All companies in Italy keep two sets of books to survive the confiscatory tax; one set to show the government and another to know what is going on. The only way they could cook the books was to keep sales and manufacturing at arm's length from each other.

In Portugal I visited two factories. After the revolution of the 1960s, the government nationalized the brewing industry which also owned the glass plants. The factories wanted me to prepare a report to support their request to the government for money to modernize.

In Greece, the management knew they had major quality problems and after they joined the common market they would be non-competitive with imports. How could they make the needed improvements to quality? I failed them, they also failed, and the plant was shut down a year later.

In Kala Lumpur, Malaysia, the Chinese quality manager, Lip Sip Tech, who I spent the day with, hosted me to dinner. Over a lobster meal, I told him, "Lip Sip Tech, I want to compliment on your English, it is very good." He generously replied, "Thank you, Bernie, it should be; it is my native tongue." We Americans can be so stupid on foreign soil. He grew up and attended school when Malaysia was a colony of England.

At a factory on the outskirts of Jakarta, Indonesia, which was adjacent to a swamp, I found one problem, that bothered a crew working in the warehouse with open sides, was the frequency of cobras they encountered between the cartons. My suggestion to employ a snake charmer did not fly.

In Glasgow, Scotland, their factory made most of the scotch bottles for their country. I was invited to attend the noon meeting of the plant manager and his three supervisors. The secretary brought in a tall drinking glass for each of us and asked our preference. Then she poured our glasses half full of scotch, straight up. We had our choice of a half dozen different bottles supplied by their customers. I found among the Scotch men, their top pick was Johnnie Walker Red Label -- at least that day. It certainly made for a relaxed meeting and a short afternoon.

I spent time in six factories in Australia, and they wanted my technical expertise. The plant in Hobart, Tasmania, was obsolete and has since been shut down. My abilities were challenged in factories in Melbourne and Brisbane that had major quality problems. At factories in Sydney and Adelaide, I felt inadequate in some respects, because they were technically ahead of us; so it was a learning experience for me. I was invited back to Australia several years in a row, because I think Sydney and Adelaide liked to hear my compliments. The Aussies are quite advanced technically, they love America, and they love Americans. Half the people I encountered had travelled in America as tourists.

I was sent to a glass factory in New Zealand that was about to be shut down, because their major customer was about to cut them off for poor quality and import glass from Japan. It is a long and complex story I will not bore you with, but I bought them time with the customer to fix their problems, and told the factory management what they had to do. I was invited back again after a year and hailed as a hero, because the plant had been successful and survived. It was similar to the story in Reims, France.

Shortly after I retired and agreed with the company president to provide consulting on a part-time basis, I was called by the General Manager of the Owens-Illinois Kimble Division that sold scientific glassware to world-wide customers. They were rapidly losing market share, the manager felt the cause may be poor quality, and asked me for an appraisal. I visited their eight factories and several sales branches, and then wrote him a report. Yes, they had major quality problems, which I identified, and then provided a five step program to turn things around. He thanked me for the report and I heard nothing for several months. I had now retired and was mowing the lawn. One noon he phoned and asked me to come to his office. I entered and he indicated a chair. "Keating, I have tried to sell the company, but no one would buy because they said we had poor quality; so I guess I will have to manage it instead. I read your report and agree with your outline of the problems and your five-step program to fix them. Are you ready to implement?" I replied, "yes." He said, "fine. I will tell all the plant managers that you report directly to me. I will not need any progress reports, because I will know what is going on. Any questions?" I responded, "no," and after this two minute meeting I left his office. I worked with his people for nearly two years, and we created a new quality culture, the first effective one the company ever had. Kimble then became identified as the top quality world-wide supplier of scientific glassware. Then the company was sold to a German company. I have mixed feelings about my success because all my friends there were now working on a German payroll.

The interesting thing I learned early in my travels was that in most factories there were people somewhere in the operation who knew what the problems were and what was needed to be done. I developed the ability to seek-out these people, listen to them, and then provide the analysis of the problem and solutions back to their own management. They thought it was my expertise, but actually I was feeding them mostly information from their own people. Perhaps I should be called a middle-man management "broker". Of course you also had to have some expertise gained from experience, and my consulting job also called for "guts and grit". Fifty years on the firing line will give you that.

Now, back to that Reims factory in France. After working in a half-dozen factories scattered through their country side, I became an expert on French cuisine. Dining with the French is more than a meal; it is an adventure. Cuisine will involve multiple courses. Let me describe the typical dinner I encountered numerous times, and you may want to replicate it when serving Coquille St. Jacques. The French love conversation to start an encounter; so a meal may start in the salon, where you serve an aperitif. A favorite is Dubonet, but it could also be sweet vermouth with a cherry or even Campari with a splash of soda.

Since I have never encountered the matter of a pre-meal blessing in France, I am not sure of the protocol for one, but perhaps in the casual atmosphere of the salon is an opportunity for you to intercede as you address the guests: *"In my anticipation of the wonderful cuisine that is to follow, may I ask the Lord to bless our meal, and give thanks for this fellowship with my family and friends. Please now raise you glass for a toast to our host par-excellence and in tribute to great French cuisine."*

Then you move to the table for the initial course of pâté. I do not lay claim to expertise in preparing this dish, but have developed a simple recipe consisting of ground fried liver mixed with sautéed leeks and some embellishments in a compressed ball. My recipe remains a work-in-process; so I would suggest you obtain a pâté from your local delicatessen. This course could be served with chilled dry vermouth served in a martini glass and if you are adventurous, add a touch of gin.

In France and also Italy, a small salad is normally served after the entrée, but this is contrary to my normal American order of things; so I would now serve a small lettuce salad with vinegar and oil, along with a goblet of chilled chardonnay wine.

The next course is a vegetable. I would suggest a couple spears of steamed asparagus lightly coated with grated cheese, and you could include broccoli, lightly swirled in butter. The glass of chardonnay may need topped off. Now it is time for a small scoop of sorbet; just enough to clear the pallet and prepare for the next course, which is the entrée.

Ah! Now we come to the Coquille St. Jacques Au Gratin, the highlight of the meal. If you are both the host and the chef, not-to-worry, the dish can be prepared in advance. Like most French cuisine, it has few ingredients and is simple to prepare. Your guests may even make reference comparing you with Julia Child. The essential ingredients are scallops, onion (or leeks), grating cheese, and a few optional embellishments. How can anything be simpler than that?

For a family of six, (or six guests) get one dozen fresh scallops at the fish market. That will be two apiece, which is adequate since it is a rich dish, and remember this is a European dinner which means portions are down-sized from the huge amounts heaped on the normal American dinner plate. Place the scallops in a frying pan, add 2 cups of white wine (I have a preference for chardonnay), and then simmer for about 15 minutes over low heat.

In a separate frying pan, add a dash of oil to a splash of water and slowly heat. Add 3 cubes of chicken bouillon. Now finely chop one large onion (or leeks). As the above is sautéed, add ¼ cup of butter, one bunch of finely chopped parsley, 6 bulbs of pressed garlic, and then sprinkle 2 tablespoons of gravy flour on top and blend in.

Now add 6 large sliced mushrooms, blend in 10 heaping spoonfuls of plain non-fat yogurt, and drain all the wine from the scallops into the mixture while continuing to sauté over a low heat. Let the above gradually become "reduced" as the remaining liquid floats into the wonderful aroma of the kitchen.

Remove the scallops from their pan and place in an 8x12 inch glass casserole. Ladle the mixture from the frying pan over the scallops. Sprinkle a **thick** layer of grating cheese on top. I use a mixture of Parmesan and Romano. Place this in the oven directly under the broiler set on high until the top becomes a wonderful "golden" brown. Watch it carefully, because the change in color happens fast -- probably less than 10 minutes. Do this in advance of the meal, and let it rest in a warming oven.

Now you are ready with a wonderful entrée of Coquille St. Jacques Au Gratin. While it is seafood and normally served with a white wine, I prefer a red because the food is quite rich and will overpower a white. I prefer a goblet of Cabernet Sauvignon.

After the entrée is completed, you can relax, because the serious eating is completed, and you can engage in casual conversation as the table is again cleared. Now for dessert; it will be very European as you pass around a platter of a half-dozen various cheeses and cut-up fruit, perhaps apple, pear, and strawberries. To accompany this traditional end for a meal, may I suggest a fine port from Portugal. It would even be appropriate to again ask the guests to raise their glasses in a toast to the wonderful time together.

Let me give one caveat about the wines I have recommended If you are dining in Reims, all these choices are preempted by champagne. This is in the Champagne province of France, which holds the exclusive world-wide use of the name "champagne", at least according to the French. If you are dining as my wife and I were when hosted by the plant manager of the glass factory that makes all their bottles, then your choice of wine for every course is preordained. It will definitely be champagne. While I normally save my champagne experiences for special occasions such as a holiday or wedding, it is appropriate for it to also accompany one of my favorite dishes: Coquille St. Jacques au Gratin.

Roger and Deke on Roger's wedding day. Background scene is overlooking Hollywood from the penthouse balcony of the famous Chateau Marmont, where the wedding was held.

These two sons are both graduates of University of Notre Dame and have MBA's, Roger from Stanford University and Deke from University of California, Davis.

TWENTY: THE GLASSMAKER

Despite a couple engineering degrees from college, the most valuable contributions to my career in industry were psychology, creative writing, and public speaking. After I became the Corporate Manager of Quality Assurance for Owens-Illinois, I suddenly found myself in demand as a public speaker representing the company. That was not because I was particularly good at the task, but because no other executive at headquarters could be coerced into doing it, and I was at the bottom of the food chain. The invitation to give a talk meant: the job of preparation, rehearsal, getting the speech material approved by the legal department, a plane ride, rental car, night in a hotel room, and back home to face a host of mail, phone calls, and problems that accumulated during the trip. All of us at the corporate level had too many of those things already on our plate; no one was interested in more of the same.

During the decade after arriving at headquarters, I delivered an average of a talk every month somewhere in the U.S. or overseas. These included: "Glass Packaging" at the Baltimore convention of FDA inspectors, "Glass Packaging" at National Convention on Product Safety in Chicago, "O-I Technology" at Coca Cola headquarters in Atlanta, Georgia; "Our New Twist-Off closure" at Pepsi headquarters in Purchase, N.Y.; National Beverage Convention in New York City; National Brewery Convention in San Antonio, Texas; 7-up headquarters in Saint Louis, Missouri; a drug company in Irvine, California; meeting of Finish Product Managers of ACI in Sydney, Australia; AVIR corporate headquarters in Milan, Italy; and Gerber headquarters in Fremont, Michigan. You get the picture.

The first request for my public speaking services was for a meeting of drug companies in Williamsburg, Virginia. There was no precedent for such a talk, so I was on my own. I gradually learned that despite whatever the main theme I was to address, I could launch from a story about the history of glass. It worked well for two reasons: I was representing the biggest and best glass company in the world, and seldom did anyone know the fascinating story of the history of glass -- it always brought something new to the party.

Here is how my glass story proceeded.

A few years ago when I was hiking over Mono Pass in the Sierra Mountains of California, I found an obsidian arrowhead, no doubt from the Mono Indians who used this trade route in ancient times. Obsidian is a black glass occurring in nature that flows from the earth in the lava fields east of the mountains.

Man first learned to make glass beads around 3500 B.C. According to legend, Phoenician merchants in the Eastern Mediterranean discovered glass accidentally when they built a huge fire on the beach and set their cooking kettles on rocks of nitrate. The fire burned hot and next morning they found small beads of glass in the sand. We don't know the truth of this legend, but we do know glass was discovered in this part of the ancient world. I have visited the Vatican Museum and seen beads from that time. Hollow glass vases date back to 1500 B.C. and were found in Mesopotamia. There is evidence of other glass making activities around this same time in Egypt, Mycenae (Greece), and China.

A major step forward occurred around 300 B.C. with the invention of the blowpipe. Now bottles could be made in which liquids could be contained by corks, and the commerce of olive oil, wine, and other products grew rapidly. During the era of the Roman Empire, glassworks flourished across Western Europe and the Mediterranean. Then the dark ages descended and glassmaking gradually became centered on the island of Murano, near Venice. Craftsmen there carefully guarded the secret of how to make glass. I have visited Murano, and the island still maintains a substantial glass industry.

During the renaissance, glass making spread to France and elsewhere. The ancestors of Daphne du Maurier, the English author and playwright of such films as *Rebecca* and *The Birds*, were glassmakers in the Loire Valley near Paris. Her book, *The Glassmaker*, traces her French ancestry and gives a vivid depiction of the French revolution. It is the best literature about glassmaking during that era.

Glass making played an important role in the early development of America. In 1607, an English company founded the settlement in Jamestown with the principle enterprise to be the manufacture of glass. The forests of England that supplied fuel for glass factories were growing scarce, so they looked at America with its endless forests where they could product glass to be shipped back to England. Further north in Massachuset, the New England Glass Company was started in 1818, and thirty years later it was recognized as the largest glass factory in the world with 500 employees. In 1872, William Libbey, who founded Owens Illinois, became part owner, and fifteen years later he moved the factory to Toledo Ohio. It was there that Michael Owens invented the automatic bottle blowing machine with the financing of Libbey. The Owens Bottle Machine Corporation was incorporated in 1907, and twenty two years later after a merger, became the Owens-Illinois Glass Company.

Today, O-I is the largest manufacturer of glass containers in North America, South America, and India, and the second largest in Europe. It has affiliates or licensees in Australia, South East Asia, China, Japan, and elsewhere in over thirty countries. Approximately one of every two glass containers made worldwide is made by Owens Illinois, its affiliates, or its licensees. It is the leader in technology, the high-productivity/low cost producer, and the leading supplier in almost all of the markets it serves. As the Corporate Manager of Quality Assurance, I was always happy to announce that we were rated as the top quality supplier of glass containers in the world.

How do you produce a glass container?

After graduating from college, I began my career in 1954 in the Oakland glass factory. The work was dirty and with little glamour. The factory had five furnaces side-by-side in a room the size of a football field. Each furnace held tons of glass in a red-hot molten pool that was five-feet-deep; it resembled a swimming pool of molten lava. Sand and other batch ingredients were dumped into one end of the furnace and gradually melted as they passed to the other end 50-feet downstream where the molten glass, at a temperature of nearly 3,000 degrees, flowed into channels called feeders. Glass flowed along the feeder out over the forming machine, where a solid stream of glass dropped down through an orifice. Shears then cut it into individual hunks of glass called *gobs*. These gobs dropped into a trough distributor that delivered them among the individual sub-sections of the bottle-forming machine. Smoke from the operations rose overhead to exhaust through claw-like ventilators atop the factory roof.

Watching the operation of the machines is fascinating. Each red-hot gob of glass traveled a six second, multi-stage journey. First, it fell into the blank mold, where the finish threads were formed and a bubble of air was blown into the center. This first molten shape was called a *parison*. The parison was carried by an inverting arm and dropped into another mold, where a tube entered the bubble and a blast of compressed air blew the molten glass outward to conform to the shape of the mold. If it was a soda mold, the molten glass took the shape of that soda bottle. A pair of tongs on a robotic arm lifted the red-hot bottle from the mold and set it onto a conveyor belt, where it traveled into an annealing lehr. As I said, this process of making a bottle took only seconds from the time the molten glass flowed from the furnace, and then the process started over, occurring simultaneously in each of the other ten sections of the machine. Some machines had molds with four cavities each, to produce multiple bottles each cycle. The hot bottles were then clustered onto a wide conveyor mat and slowly cooled as they passed through the lehr, exiting onto other conveyors in the packing room, where a crew will inspect and pack the bottles into cartons or bulk loads..

Even with the brief background in engineering I had picked up at Berkeley, I was able to appreciate the complexity of this manufacturing process and to marvel at the interplay of simplicity with complexity. The glass-making process was as old as Western civilization itself; not much different from when the Phoenicians and Egyptians did it thousands of years before Christ. The new complexities were how to melt rail-car loads of sand into a fluid of 3,000 degrees inside furnaces that operated continuously day and night, and how to create bottle shapes in a machine that spewed out a product at the rate of hundreds per minute. Some machines produced bottles at a rate of nearly 5,000 per hour. The Oakland factory produced three million bottles per day, operating 24 hours and 7 days per week. Each furnace will operate continuously for many years until it is idled to have refractory walls replaced.

Why glass bottles and jars? Because they are the container of consumer choice around the world for many products. Glass is recyclable, nearly inert, it can be molded into many shapes, is chemically non-corrosive, can be made air-tight to provide integrity to a wide range of products, and it gives an aesthetically pleasing and healthy image to the consumer.

Regardless of the subject I was to address with a particular audience, I always managed to weave in part of this story of glass. I found it was always well received. Then I caught the plane home for another busy day in the office. Now retired after a fifty year career, I think this may be the last time I have to address the story of glass.

Roger and Lou Wedding in 2005 held in the Penthouse of Chateau Marmont, Hollywood. From the left, Sarah Thornton, Monte Thornton, Glenda Thornton, Lou, Roger, Aurdery, Lorie, Treci, Deke, and me.

TWENTY ONE: AN ITALIAN FEAST

Yes, I know spaghetti was originally a Chinese dish, because it was invented there during the era of Kublai Khan, when the Italian Marco Polo travelled to China and brought the dish back home to Italy; but don't bother to explain that to my wife, who is of Italian ancestry. Spaghetti is Italian! However, you could make the case that Marco Polo was not even Italian. I have visited the home where he was born; it isn't even in Italy. It is on the island of Korcula on the Adriatic Sea in the country of Croatia. Of course, a history buff would explain that Krocula was part of Italy when Marco Polo lived there; so whether or not spaghetti has Italian ancestry, it has certainly become Italian by adoption, and I know of no Chinese who lay claim to the dish.

I am not a huge fan of spaghetti; however, I have a large craving for spaghetti sauce. I place a very small mound of spaghetti on my plate and cover it with a huge ladle of spaghetti sauce. Then I lather grating cheese on top. That procedure is particularly true if it is the fabulous sauce that I personally manufacture. I have a recipe that is absolutely phenomenal, and it should be; it is as Italian as paddy's pig is Irish.

I should know Italian. In addition to marrying a beautiful lady of Italian ancestry, I have four children who are half Italian. Moreover, I have travelled Italy from one-end-to the other numerous times and have eaten the food that each of its regions lay claim to. My first visits were business trips when I was providing technical assistance to glass factories around the country, and then later I returned as a tourist and also to visit my daughter who was a naval officer stationed at the NATO base in Naples.

For a country that has spread its people and culture world-wide, Italy is surprisingly insular and keeps within a narrowly defined space, keeping its secrets to itself.

This from my wife: "Don't you dare reveal Nono's (her father's) secret spaghetti sauce recipe to anyone!"

"No, Dear, I won't. I will only talk about the recipe that I invented myself." In fact, Nono's sauce was different every time he made it, because the ingredients always changed. The one I will reveal is my own, invented by me -- not the Chinese or the Italians -- and while it also is not Irish, it is relished by my children who share an Italian/Irish ancestry.

People speak of Italian cuisine, but that is somewhat a misnomer. Their food is uniquely different in each of the various regions, and the locals give intense loyalty to their own creations. It is somewhat like describing typical American food for someone from South Dakota as grits, and black eyed peas. I have never tasted grits or black eyed peas and I am American. The ante pasta served in Piedmont is completely different from that served in Lombardy or Bari. My wife's ancestry is Piedmonte, and her loyalty is to that food, but she will tolerate the food from Modena, where her father's ancestry comes from.

Let's get started with the recipe for my sauce. When I make it every couple months, I make a huge batch and freeze part of it, which will come in handy when company arrives and I have little time for cooking. Now let me give a surprise opener. Go to the store and purchase three 48 ounce jars of Ragu Traditional Spaghetti Sauce. Relax. It is only a background base ingredient. I find Ragu sauce has excellent flavor but is too thin to be really good. I visited the Ragu plant in Buffalo, New York,

118

when I was in the bottle business and they were one of my customers. They are a quality organization and make an excellent product, even though it is too thin for my liking, so I use it only as background starting material.

In a very large kettle, add some canola oil, water, and heat. Then add the following:

3 large chopped onions

3 or 4 chopped carrots

10 bulbs of garlic

A finely chopped bunch of parsley

Oregano and other Italian seasoning

Salt and pepper

In a large frying pan cook:

3 pounds of ground sirloin

1 pound of sausage

Add this to the kettle. Now add the three jars of Ragu, 2 cups of red wine, stir, and simmer for an hour. Pour off what you can devour over the next couple days in a refrigerator jar, and then put the remainder back into the empty Ragu jars and place in the freezer. Mushrooms should be added to the sauce as it is warmed up, but do not add prior to freezing.

Now for the spaghetti. In the same large kettle that is now empty, fill it with hot water; add salt and a splash of canola oil. When the water comes to a boil, add the spaghetti and keep the water boiling. After ten minutes start to sample, and while the spaghetti is still "el dente", declare it ready. Pour the contents through a colander with the water going down the sink. Place the drained spaghetti back in the warm, empty kettle and stir in some sauce that will prevent sticking. Let it rest in the kettle until it is time to place it on a platter to be served.

If you want to be really Italian, and even Piedmonteze, then serve ante pasta like it is done in the town of Asti in the Piedmont providence.

Prepare some green onions, strips of red pepper, stalks of celery, perhaps a couple bulbs of broccoli, cauliflower, a couple mushrooms, and several slices of dry salami. Into an individual bowl on each plate, pour some olive oil and red wine vinegar, salt and pepper. Arrange the vegetables on the plate surrounding the bowl.

Now we are ready to start the Italian meal. There will be three courses: ante pasta, pasta, and dessert. After calling the guests to the table, the host will begin with a blessing. Since this is Italian, a Catholic grace would be appropriate:

> **Bless us oh Lord**
> **And these thy gifts**
> **Which we are about to receive**
> **From thy bounty**
> **Through Christ our Lord.**   **Amen**

At each place setting there will be two empty wine goblets and one demitasse. Into one goblet pour some chardonnay. Then the host should propose a toast:

> **We toast the Italian Gods,**
> **Who have prepared this great feast.**

Then start the ante pasta. The true Italian will swirl the vegetables in the bowl and eat. This is finger-food; remember it is an Italian meal.

After the ante pasta, the bowls are removed and a platter of spaghetti is placed on the table in front of the male host. The ritual is that each person will pass their plate to him and utilizing two very large forks, he will ladle spaghetti onto each plate, which is then passed back to the person where it came from. As the host is dropping spaghetti onto plates, people will provide instructions or comments such as:

Oh! That is too much; I must save room for later.
It looks wonderful; another forkful, please.
Looks wonderful and I will be back again later for
more.

At the beginning of the pasta course, without fanfare, fill the second wine goblet with Cabernet Sauvignon. A bowl with the sauce is passed around. Place a heaping amount of sauce on the spaghetti, and then sprinkle on top a liberal portion of Parmesan and Romano grating cheese.

How do you get the squirrely spaghetti from the plate to your mouth? For openers, you do **not** roll a forkful against a spoon. That is Irish. You simply place a goodly amount on the end of the fork, twist the fork to secure it firmly, bend your head toward the plate, and shovel it in. If a strand does not make it all the way, politely suck it in. Remember, this is an Italian meal. Use your napkin frequently to daub the sauce from your lips.

Now we are ready for the third course: dessert. Everyone is stuffed at this point, so dessert is a nibbling process as the conversation turns to a discussion about some cousin who is not present to defend himself. A plate is passed around the table that contains three cheeses and several pieces of cut-up fruit. For cheeses, I suggest sharp cheddar, and two other imported Italian cheeses. The fruit could be apple, pear, and strawberries.

The demitasse is now filled with a fine imported port from Portugal. Pause and in a humble voice, modestly ask the guests to raise their glasses in a toast:

To the chef and his fabulous spaghetti sauce. Salute.

Nona and Noni, Aurdery's parents. Nona was born in Bloomington, Indiana, of parents who came to America from Turino, Italy. Noni was born in Delzel, Illinois, and is a second generation Italian, his father having emigrated from Modena, Italy.

Wedding photo of Aurdery's parents (on the right side) in the early 1920s. On the left are Nona's brother, John Buffo, who was Best Man, and his first wife, Hilldred.

TWENTY TWO: TCHAIKOVSKY AND I

Some of my favorite music is composed by Tchaikovsky. Shortly after Aurdery and I were married, we took a class together entitled Music Appreciation at a local college. The format was to focus each week on a piece of music in considerable detail and gain an appreciation for its musical development and why it had such a special impact on listeners. One of the "cause célèbre" was the Fifth Symphony of Tchaikovsky. During all the many years since, this musical work has been one of my favorites. The second movement in particular is especially gifted; well crafted, colorfully orchestrated, and with a memorable solo for the French horn, one of the best in all of music.

Who can say why some particular piece of music has such a personal impact? I pondered this question and perhaps there is a connection between the orchestrated gyrations of this musical work and my work-a-day life in the glass factory. The music involves a long struggle, noise, repetition, complexity, controversy, and success ultimately at the end. The Fifth is a cyclical symphony, with a recurring main theme, which is heard in all four movements. It starts with a funereal character in the first movement, but gradually transforms into a triumphant march, which dominates to the end. The musical theme development is thought to experience "providence" -- divine guidance -- and expresses the idea of ultimate victory through strife. Perhaps this is why this Russian symphony was popular during the long struggle of World War II as we fought toward victory. The word "fate" comes to mind.

The other evening I was home alone, while my wife was visiting her sister in Fresno. I put Tchaikovsky's Fifth on the stereo and sat down with a glass of wine. The music started. As my eyes glazed over, I found myself in a twilight zone somewhere between the music and days-gone-by; I was back again in the glass factory.

FIRST MOVEMENT: andante - allegro con anima. It is moderately slow and a ponderous statement, yet with vitality and excitement. I find it to be confusing: moderately slow and even; yet brisk, lively, sprightly, walking, and cheerful with animation. Yes, it is all those things in a mixed bag, much like my day of work in the glass factory. I am walking into the factory now. It is 6:30 a.m. as I am enveloped by the tumult of the factory: clanking of metal on metal of the bottle machines, blasts of compressed air, grinding of conveyor belts, whine of air fans, phones ringing, bottles clanking against each other; all in a rising crescendo -- trumpets come in as the recurring theme of "fate" goes over-and-over; now an octave higher. The B1 production shop roars as the bottles get dumped into a cullet chute. As I walk down the production lines, I see problems: machine problems, people problems -- my problems. I hear the harmonic overtones: trumpets, violas, oboes, bassoons, clarinets, and cellos -- all in dissonance-- piccolos barely discernible above the violins, and then the tympanis. The music grows faster and more energetic, but remains dark and apprehensive, occasionally punctuated by loud, violent outbursts. It is as if fate is coming after me with every foreboding, malevolent tool in its bag: union threats, uncontrolled costs, a strike, another mass worker layoff. At last I reach my office and close the door. I am in my safe sanctuary. The music fades as the movement come to an end.

SECOND MOVEMENT: andante cantabile, con alcuna licenza - moderato con anima. It starts slow and even, liberating, vital, liveliness, sprightliness, veracity, excitement, gay, songlike, flowing, and singing. The tender, haunting, expressive solo melody played by the French horn resonates with passion. Now I am retired, elderly, and living in comfort as I think again about those yesteryears in the glass factory. Things are going fine; at least for now. I cherish the fond memories of Ray, Charley, and Dick, and the comradeship we shared for so many years. Ed's funeral comes back to me with the haunting dirge of the French horn, underpinned with the deep baritone of the double bass played an octave lower and grumbling in counterpoint. Yes I am at peace with my memories.

Then suddenly my reverie is shattered as the music roars its turbulence as if fate is calling me back, and I am unable to escape my protagonist. I am again with the unrelenting roar of the glass factory; I am brought again to reality. The music rises in a crescendo, and slowly fades away.

THIRD MOVEMENT: valse, allegro moderate. The music starts with a graceful pastoral waltz and I am again in my sanctuary office with the door closed and slowly I read the mail. I have temporarily escaped from fate's cruel clutches. My secretary blocks the door and will re-direct all my phone calls. It is a moment of quiet and of peace. I quietly slip out my back door and head to the warehouse, and walk up and down the empty corridors with my mind elsewhere in a refreshing diversion from the cares of the factory. But there are musical overtones suggesting a quiet statement of the fate theme that is both innocuous and ominous. Try as I might, my protagonist-self cannot escape destiny. I return to my office and there sits Carlos -- the union president -- waiting for me. He is angry with me and with the company and with the world, and he lets me know in unmentionable terms. There is no accommodation, no compromise; only confrontation. The music reacts with a loud crash of cymbals, roll of the base drums, horns blaring; I can see the maestro on his podium, hair flowing, swinging wildly at the orchestra, and he brings the music to a close with unrelenting finality and angry arms.

FOURTH MOVEMENT: finale, andante maestoso - allegro vivace. Tchaikovsky transposes the fate theme from the dusky moody key of E Minor to the bright sunshine of E major in a majestic and stately walk through my yet-to-come years of retirement. Trumpets, flutes, and stings of the violin are singing to me. I am inside the glass factory as I wave goodbye to my secretary and walk through the exit door for the last time. It is as if Tchaikovsky is walking alongside and telling me that we cannot escape from our destiny; but can overcome my circumstances -- the hard work, the daily grind -- and turn them into something brighter and better. He gives me this universal theme through his music, and he is telling me it can be applied to my life. Just as his music is lifting me up and carrying me to new heights, I am reminded that fate is in my own hands.

The music comes to an end, but I remain with eyes closed and ponder again the musical friendship of Tchaikovsky and his symphony.

Roger, Lou, Cooper and Lilah during their vacation in 2009

The Englhardt family at Thanksgiving in 2009 when they were with us in Sonora. Front row: Zachary and Carson, and back row: Addison, Eric, Lorie, and McKenna.

Deke at his 44th birthday party in Sonora in 2010. He is such an excellent cook that we made him cook the meal

TWENTY THREE : MY GREEK CONNECTION

μήτηρ γάρ τέ μέ φησι θεὰ Θέτις ἀργυρόπεζα
διχθαδίας κῆρας φερέμεν θανάτοιο τέλος δέ.
εἰ μέν κ' αὖθι μένων Τρώων πόλιν ἀμφιμάχωμαι,
ὤλετο μέν μοι νόστος, ἀτὰρ κλέος ἄφθιτον ἔσται
εἰ δέ κεν οἴκαδ' ἵκωμι φίλην ἐς πατρίδα γαῖαν,
ὤλετό μοι κλέος ἐσθλόν, ἐπὶ δηρὸν δέ μοι αἰὼν
ἔσσεται, οὐδέ κέ μ' ὦκα τέλος θανάτοιο κιχείη.

Perhaps you prefer an English translation:

*For my mother <u>Thetis</u> the goddess of silver feet tells me
I carry two sorts of destiny toward the day of my death.
Either, if I stay here and fight beside the city of the Trojans,
my return home is gone, but my glory shall be everlasting;
but if I return home to the beloved land of my fathers,
the excellence of my glory is gone, but there will be a long
life left for me, and my end in death will not come to me
quickly.*

You can now claim to have read part of Homer's epic poem, the Iliad, and read it both in the English translation and also in Homer's original Greek. The Iliad is set in the Trojan War, the ten year siege of a coalition of Greek states; it tells of the battles and events. Homer's Odyssey is in part a sequel to the Iliad. If you have a Greek son-in-law who was educated in Greek schools, as I have, he will be able to tell you all about these two epic tales by Homer. He can also describe all the Greek Gods and tell you the mythology associated with each, he can tell you about his Greek Orthodox religious faith, and if Greek music is on the radio he will jump to his feet in a display of Zorba the Greek, and will teach you the hypnotic ten-step dance with his arms on your shoulders encircling your own.

Greece is one of the few countries in the world where folk dances are as alive today as they were in ancient times. Dance has always played an important role in their life; it is an expression of human feelings and everyday life. The Greeks dance at religious festivals and ceremonies; they dance to ensure fertility, and to celebrate victories; they dance at weddings, to overcome depression, and to cure physical illness. It is glue that bonds their community, and is central to the Hellenic culture; folk dancing has been a unifying part of the culture.

Everyone should experience a three-day Greek Festival, as I just did, and become immersed in a microcosm of Greek culture with loud music, endless dancing, a myriad of Greek foods, and rubbing shoulders as you listen to conversations that become intermingled with English and Greek. It is an experience unlike any other, and the Greek Festival in America is symbolic of the world-wide best in ethnic cultures. Greek-Americans are proud to become naturalized American citizens, and also proud to remain citizens of the Greek homeland. They did not give-up the old life and loyalties as they embraced their new life and the U.S. Pledge of Allegiance.

That is how it was with my son-in-law, George, when he emigrated to America with his visa at the age of twenty-five to marry my daughter. She is a naval officer whose first duty station was at an American naval base in Greece, where she began dating George, and one thing led to another. Today they have three children, one in elementary school, one in high school, and one in college. She remains on active duty in the navy, and he continues with his twenty-year career as an electrician on U.S. Navy bases. They have two homes: one in Virginia where they both work, and one in Greece where they spend time each year.

In addition to religion and dancing, another thing central to Greek culture is their food. At the festival you can get all the specialties: loukoumades, Greek salad, moussaka, tiropita, pastitsio, spanakopita, chicken lathoregano, gyro, calamari, souvlaki, rice pilaf, shish kebab, and baklava for dessert. Perhaps you may start with a sip of ouzo, and highlight the meal with a bottle of Greek wine.

My favorite Greek meal is a skewer of shish kebab served on a bed of rice pilaf. It is a meal that is common to all countries of the Eastern Mediterranean. Like all the recipes of that region, it originated in Ancient Greece before the time of Alexandra the Great, and then was recycled through the civilizations that followed: Roman, Byzantine, Turk, Ottoman Empire, and back again to modern Greece.

Shish kebab is so basic that it has changed little during the past three millennium. It is meat on a skewer interspersed with various vegetables, and it is best cooked over a campfire or BBQ grill. It is the ultimate for a macho male who fanaticizes he is struggling for survival against the Trojans, and needs a goblet of cabernet sauvignon to maintain strength for the undertaking.

Our daughter, Captain Treci Dimas USN, whose first duty station after being commissioned in 1981 was in Nea Makri, Greece. She met George Dimas, and they started dating. They were married in 1984 in Toledo, OH.

Dimas family: Alexandra, Treci, Angela, George, and Ari. This was Angela's graduation from high school, and she is all dressed up for her senior prom night.

133

TWENTY FOUR: CAMPING VACATIONS

AND what is so rare as a day in June?
Then, if ever, come perfect days;
Then heaven tries earth if it be in tune,
And over it softly her warm ear lays;
Whether we look, or whether we listen,
We hear life murmur, or see it glisten;
Every clod feels a stir of might,
An instinct within it that reaches and towers,
And, groping blindly above it for light,
Climbs to a soul in grass and flowers;
The flush of life may well be seen
Thrilling back over hills and valleys;
The cowslip startles in meadows green,
The buttercup catches the sun in its chalice,
And there's never a leaf nor a blade too mean
To be some happy creature's palace;
The little bird sits at his door in the sun,
Atilt like a blossom among the leaves,
And lets his illuminated being o'errun
With the deluge of summer it receives;
His mate feels the eggs beneath her wings,

And the heart in her dumb breast flutters and sings;
He sings to the wide world, and she to her nest,
In the nice ear of Nature which song is the best? [11]

Ah! June, open air, and nature on a beautiful spring day; and that means you should grab a blanket, frying pan, and head into the woods. I've done it all my life. To earn my Boy Scout Camping Merit Badge, I had to spend several dozen such nights. I have camped everywhere. When I was in the navy; I continued the tradition. While in Wonson harbor, North Korea, conducting shore bombardment, I was assigned as officer-in-charge of a shore party to go to Yo Do Island that was occupied by British Commandoes, and man a searchlight atop a hill that provided azimuths for navy planes to find their way back to their aircraft carrier in the dark of night. That camping experience meant spending the nights in sleeping bags alongside slit trenches in the event of incoming fire.

When my ship returned to the San Diego, I often spent a night in the fancy lounges of Palm Springs, then driving into the desert and sleeping alongside my car rolled up in a navy blanket. On a three day holiday weekend with no money, my shipmate buddy, Buck Rogers, and I headed to Ensenada, Mexico, where we ate ten-cent tacos from street vendors, drank ten-cent beer in the dance taverns, and then headed to the beach and rolled up in navy blankets. Sleeping on the beach is an unpleasant experience. The second night we headed out of town, found a flat field in the darkness, and rolled up in blankets on the ground beside the car. When the sun rose, we found ourselves camping on the end of the runway of Ensenada Airport. We did a hasty departure.

In keeping with this tradition, shortly after Aurdery and I were married, we headed to Carmel for a weekend. After dinner in a restaurant, I drove up the wild and unsettled Carmel Canyon, found a meadow in the darkness, and parked the car.

"That looks like a nice place to camp for the night," I announced to Aurdery.

"What do you mean?" She asked. "You have got to be kidding," she responded rather curtly. "I am not going to sleep out there in the wild!"

So I headed back to Carmel and began looking for a suitable vacant lot, but there are no vacant lots in Carmel. At midnight, we found a parking spot and spent the night. Needless to say, the next morning we checked into a motel in Carmel. That was the end of my youth-time camping tradition.

A dozen years later after we had a family, our children announced to me that they wanted to go camping like all their neighbor friends. In true macho male fashion, I responded, "You will have to ask your Mother." So with the help of four kids, the deal was consummated, but I knew there were four inviolate caveats:

1. We'd have to have the best camping equipment that money could buy.
2. My wife could never be asked to cook when camping.
3. All dishes must be disposable with no washing, other than a Dutch oven, frying pan and coffee pot.
4. There must be sanitary toilet facilities and water available.

True to my word in forty years of camping, I have never asked Aurdery to cook a meal or wash a pot, pan, or any dishes. I made the big purchases: two tents, folding cot for everyone, sleeping bags, ice box, propane stove, and lanterns. From the beginning with Deke still in diapers, our children loved it. The first camping trip was to Custer State Park in South Dakota near my home town. We started the tradition of hiking and climbing mountains; the first one was Harney Peak in the Black Hills. That was in 1968, and over the next forty years we camped in the following places:

Custer State Park, SD - 3 times

Rocky Mtn. Nat. Park, CO - 3 times

Lake Tahoe State Park, CA - 3 times

Tuolumne Meadows, Yosemite, years in 1970s - 4 times.

Tuolumne Meadows, Yosemite, years in 2000+ - 6 times

Cape Anne, MA - 2 times

Cape Cod, MA - 1 time

Adirondack Mtn., NY - 3 times

Put-in-Bay, Lake Erie, OH - 1 time

Black Lake, MI - 2 times

Manistique, MI - 1 time

Sunset Beach, CA, - 4 times

White Mtn., NH - 1 time

Yellowstone Nat. Park, WY - 1 time

Fort Bragg, CA - 1 time

Trinity Alps, CA - 1 time

Mt. Lassen, CA - 1 time

Stanislaus Nat. Forest, CA - 6 times

Sonora Pass, CA - 2 times

Deer hunting, CA - 5 times

Edison Lake, CA - 2 times

And we still camp. Every year on Labor Day, Aurdery and I are joined by son, Deke, for a week of camping, hiking, and mountain climbing in Tuolumne Meadows, Yosemite.

Almost every campsite we visited in the United States was adjacent to an ocean beach, a lake, or a mountain stream. We always stayed away from the highway and the transient camping crowd. In all the years, we never encountered a single bad incident with another camper nor ever had a single piece of equipment turn up missing. We found that family campers universally are good people.

While it was never a consideration, camping is also the most economical vacation available. I recently did a rough calculation and estimate I now have an additional $250,000 investment portfolio I would not have except for camping with my family. That certainly helps supplement my retirement income.

Why do we camp? I don't know the answer. Perhaps it carries us back to our roots when our ancestors came across the country in covered wagon, or some other such experience; we find ourselves as pioneers again. Why does the macho male stand over a smoking BBQ in the open air to cook a steak? Why? It gives him a strong feeling of masculine pride. "I may be a modern man, but damn it, I am a MAN!"

Panning for gold on Iron Creek in the Black Hills. This was 1969 and we were camping at Stockade Lake near Custer. We did not find any gold, but we did catch some trout.

Deke fishing below the Tuolumne Meadows waterfall.

The same camping trip to the Black Hills where we were gold panning in Iron Creek. This was at Stockade Lake near Custer. Of all the camping experiences, we look back at this as one of our best.

The Englhardt family on their climb up Harney Peak in the summer of 2008. We reached the top just as it became apparent a storm was brewing, so we headed quickly down. Five minutes later the storm hit, and it was the most violent lightning and thunder storm I have ever witnessed at ground level. I was frightened for our safety, but it gave the kids something to talk about for the rest of their lives.

Aurdery and I in Tuolumne Meadows last year. Our first year camping in Tuolumne Meadows in Yosemite National Park was in 1970. Our family vacation consisted or two weeks, the first at this campsite, and a second week on the beach at Sunset State Park near Capitola.

In the 40 years since 1970, we have camped near this same campsite now ten times, and again last year with Deke.

TWENTY FIVE: CONCERTO IN LYELL CANYON

Tuolumne Meadows at the 9000 feet elevation in Yosemite National Park, has been the site of our annual family camping adventure every since our kids emerged from diapers. With them grown and scattered to the winds, the annual sojourn is now down to my wife, one adult son, and me. I almost cancelled this year, because I was not up-to-snuff with some gout; but came anyway, ready for some scaled-down activities. This morning I opted for a "girlie" program, which was a writer's workshop. I am not normally chauvinistic, but somehow on this particular day, perhaps because I felt demoted to a program with only women, I did develop a rather macho attitude.

The ranger guide was Carol, who led last night's camp fire program. She was a writer, too, announcing that she wrote exactly three pages every morning to start her day. "Oh no", I thought to myself, "Not one of those obsessive writer types."

She said the program today will be two hours of hiking interspersed with writing. The class consisted or her, two ladies, and me. She explained we would hike for a half hour, write for twenty minutes, hike for another half hour, and then write for twenty minutes. The first session would focus on a "microscopic" view of nature, and the second on the "macroscopic." She handed each of us a magnifying glass and off we went.

First stop was to look at some exotic species of a mushroom, which we were invited to examine with our magnifying glass and note the web-like structures. The two ladies expressed delight as they turned the mushroom over-and-over to discover the microscopic world. We continued on. The ranger placed her nose against a pine tree to smell the aroma of its bark and invited us to do the same. I had smelled the bark of Jeffery pine trees with their scent of vanilla many times before, but did it anyway. She found a small plant alongside the trail and invited us to rub our fingers on the leaves, taking care not to bruise them, and then smell our fingers. I did and correctly identified it as something like mint, and she was delighted that I was participating. "Yes," she announced, "it is a species of mint." She continued on, bending over to view the pine cones that littered the trail, and picked up a bulb, which she broke apart and blew against it so we could see the hundreds of seeds on parachutes that flew off into the wind. I did not want to disappoint her, so I exclaimed "wow" with as much enthusiasm as I could muster.

Then she invited us to find a log to sit on and spend the next twenty minutes writing about the little things of our "microscopic" world.

What to write? I was sure it would not be very good on such short notice. I spotted a dead pine tree with a knurled trunk that swirled upward in a spiral, like something from a geometry class. So I had an opening line -- all that is needed to start a dissertation.

THE SPIRALED TREE
The spiral swirling up the trunk of the knurled pine tree caught my eye and focused my thoughts on another spiral -- the double helix of my own genome. Then I realized all the nature around me, the ant climbing up the log, the lupine flower, the pine tree, they each have a spiral helix of their own individual genome.

Genome," what a coarse, crude sounding name for something fundamental to all of nature, and also to each of us. Yes, that ant climbing up the log has its own spiral helix in every one of its cells; and scientists tell us the ant is my tenth cousin, twice removed, and if we were to examine the spiral staircase of its cells, maybe its genome is somewhat like our own.

Does this provide me with a clue to why nature is so personal, so imitatively intertwined with our own inner being? Way back there somewhere in our past, we shared the same root stock; that ant, that knurled pine tree with the spiral on its trunk, and me – an old knurled guy.

No matter, we can love nature simply for what it is -- a tenth cousin twice removed, or not -- because it does touch our inner being, and carries us outward to a wondrous world.

Then the twenty minutes were up, and we were invited to read our renditions. The lady with the pink shorts read first. It was a paragraph with a theme that escaped me. The other lady declined to read. I read mine. I question they even knew what a genome was, nor cared, certainly nothing they could see under a magnifying glass. "Fine" the ranger said as I finished, and she smiled. It was time to move on.

We hiked another half hour and arrived at a beautiful meadow in Lyell Canyon alongside a clear flowing stream. Overhead was Mammoth Mountain, which she announced she had climbed the previous day. It is a huge, foreboding mountain, rounded on top, no established trails, so seldom climbed by anyone other than a ranger. Further to the north were Mount Gibbs and Mount Dana, both of which I had climbed. Mount Dana is over 12,000 feet in elevation, and I climbed it thirty years ago with three of my children when they were all pre-teens. The ranger invited us to find a place to sit and write for twenty minutes about our setting with a "macroscopic" theme.

That morning, I had read a story by Louis L'Amour, and his opening line was, "A vast sky arched blue and empty to the horizon." No one is better at opening lines than Louis L'Amour, so I was ready to begin my dissertation.

LYELL CANYON

The vast sky arched blue and empty to the horizon. Soft shadows of lodge pole pines cast their spell along the cliffs of Mammoth Mountain and down among the coolness of Lyell Canyon, where the creek cascaded on toward its ocean destination; and left me here alone to ponder the stillness of life in the meadow, and its contrast to the life I left behind in the city.

Even the drone of the airplane overhead failed to spoil the beauty of the cascading creek singing its melody -- now the viola with its deeply throated sound, then the tympanis as rapids played off the embankment, and above it all the violins of wind blowing through the swaying pines.

It is an orchestra, and I am the conductor. No baton have I, only my eyes to take in the blush of green sedges, grasses bending to the breeze, and my ears to hear the stellar jay atop the trees complaining to the wind that robs it of dinner; and yes, as a harmonic, there is the cascading brook. It is all in tune with the cadence of nature.

Would I, the conductor, have a baton, I would change nothing, only motion to the breeze to continue its hypnotic beat, and I close my eyes and listen to this concerto of Lyell Canyon.

Again, we were invited to read our renditions. The lady in shorts read a long story telling how this creek flowed over rocks and through containment dams, to its ultimate destination, the ocean. (How could she write that much in only twenty minutes?) The other lady again declined to read, announcing that her stuff was too political. I smiled and said, "That must be Sierra Club stuff"? She even smiled as she responded, "No, much more political than that." Few things could be more political in this setting, but I let the subject drop. The ranger read her rendition. I guess she did not have her three-page warm up this morning, because her story missed it mark, whatever its mark was intended to be.

Then I read mine. "Fine", the ranger announced, and smiled. The class was finished, and we traded the usual thank you and goodbyes. I quickly headed back to civilization, leaving the two ladies in the care of the ranger.

What had I learned about writing? Perhaps nothing, or if nothing more, at least a continued appreciation that Louis L'Amour does write a good opening line.

The houses at the Cuyhoga Gold Mine on the side of Iron Mountain and a mile south of Mt Rushmore. The one in the foreground was my Dad's home from the time he arrived in the Black Hills with his father and younger brother, Elmer, until he left as a teenager to work in other mines in the Black Hills.

Work crew at Cuyhoga Gold Mine. Owner, Mr. Gira (my Dad's uncle - by marriage) is in center, and Sylvester Gira (Dad's cousin) is 2nd from left. Not in the picture is my granddad (Dad's father) -- someone had to work while these guys loafed.

The Gira's lived in Custer and Sylvester had two boys in Custer High School the same age as Denis and Edwin.

TWENTY SIX: MEDITERRANEAN CUISINE

O SOLE MIO
(You are my sunlight)

Chebella cosa 'naiurnata'e sole,
N'aria serena doppo 'na tempesta
Pe'li'aria fresca pare gi'a festa,
Che bella cosa 'na iurnata's sole! [12]

You will remember the song better in English.
What a beautiful thing is a sunny day.
The air is serene after a storm
But another sun,
That's brighter still.

It's my own sun
That's upon your face!
The sun, my sun
It's upon your face!
It's upon your face!

What is more pleasing than beauty, sunshine, gorgeous people, a sea breeze, and Mediterranean cuisine with healthy food? "A modern construction of publicists preaches what is thought to be a healthy diet by invoking a stereotype of healthy people on the shores of the Mediterranean, and their colleagues in those countries are only too willing to perpetuate this myth. The fact-of-the-matter is that the Mediterranean region contains varied cultures and cuisines." [13] Is there such a thing as Greek Cuisine? In other words, are there ways of cooking which is uniquely Greek and not borrowed from neighboring countries, such as Italy or Turkey -- or visa versa? Yes. Greek cuisine is one of the most ancient traditions in the world and the Romans, Italians, Turks, and other civilizations that came along later borrowed from them as they crafted their own cooking traditions.

Greek cuisine is the oldest European tradition that persists today. "It is over 25 centuries old. When the uncivilized inhabitants of Europe knew nothing other than roasting meat 2500 years ago, the Greeks already knew how to mix and combine various ingredients and spices so that food was tasty and satisfying." [14]

Prior to the time of Homer and his legends of the Iliad and Odyssey, roast meat was the primary way of cooking; however, as early as the Archaic Period, two centuries before the Classic Age, Greek cooking technique began to develop. Cooking utensils developed at that time contributed to the culinary arts. "By the fifteenth century B.C., the Athenian manner was fairly select and contained a variety of recipes. They kept and fattened geese, ate venison, wild boar, fish, and fried foods in olive oil, and seasoned foods with aromatic herbs. They liked seafood such as lobsters, oysters, shrimp, prawns, sea urchins, and mussels. In addition to their regular fruit, they had a preference for figs from Attica, apples from Euboea, quines from Corinth, dates from Phoenicia, and prunes from Syria. Bread in Ancient Athens was as good as ours is today. Olives kept in brine were considered a good hors d'oeuvre. They consumed vast quantities of honey and milk and drank mugs of wine." [15] From the time of Alexandra the Great and onwards, Greek cooking became a real art. Professional cooks made their appearance at that time. They were free men (not slaves) and were generously compensated by the wealthy that employed them. Culinary schools were established to teach the art of cooking and food preparation. One had to attend the school for two years, pass difficult examinations and only then was one considered fit for employment." [16] All this occurred in ancient Greece.

Now we move to the Romans. After the art of cooking had already reached its zenith in Greece, the Romans were still satisfied with coarse, primitive simplicity in their eating habits. When they first came in contact with the Greeks, the Romans had neither choice nor variety in the selection and preparation of their foods. Their sole dish was a kind of thick soup, known as "pulmentum" made from stone-ground wheat in a type of gruel. However, the Romans became the victors over the Greeks and occupied their land. Then they began to appreciate the Greek way of life and made radical changes in their own. They brought Greek chefs to Italy and began making use of the Grecian way of cooking and there was demand for cooks from the Greek cities of Sicily. The Romans, like the "newly rich" of today, wanted to sample every known existing food: the snail, the African ostrich, wild boar of Asia, African antelope, exotic birds of Scythum, hares, deer, tortoises, and wild beasts. [17]

So the Roman cuisine became Hellenized. This cuisine then became Byzantine after Emperor Constantine the Great transferred the capital from Rome to Byzantium on the shores of the Bosporus. Not only did the patricians who followed the Roman Emperor adopt the Hellenistic dishes in their mansions, but also the rest of the population made use of the Hellenistic cuisine. [18]

Then the Turks arrived on the scene. "They were nomadic barbarians of Asia whose ancestors -- the Huns -- used to seat themselves on the flesh of their newly killed animal, which they placed between their mounts and saddle to warm and soften it so it could be consumed more easily, since they ate it raw." [19] The Turks invaded the rich, fertile areas of Asia Minor and in time adopted themselves somewhat to the way of living and customs of Byzantine inhabitants. They also absorbed their way of cooking.

Now we turn to Italian cuisine. After the fall of the Roman Empire and the invasion from the north of Germanic tribes, the dreary Dark Ages prevailed over much of Europe. An exception was in the areas of Southern Italy which remained under Byzantine rule where people adhered to most of their traditions handed down by ancestors in such towns as Naples, Bari, and Amalfi; or in Northern cities of Genoa, Pisa, or Venice which continued to trade with Constantinople. One example of the continued influence of Byzantine in Italy, concerns a lady who came to Venice from the shores of the Bosporus to marry a son of the "Doges, who ruled Venice. She brought with her fine silver and gold tableware and some valuable cutlery. Her people had used these for eating rather than eat with their hands. This was the first introduction of silver ware in the West. Until this time of the renaissance it was the custom for Italians and others in Western Europe to eat with their hands.

During the eleventh and twelfth centuries, the Italians conquered the Aegean Islands, Crete, and the islands of the Ionian Sea, and there gradually began to appear recipes bearing Italian names, although the country known as Italy did not unite until the 19th century. Later, the Turks conquered the Balkans and Asia Minor, and recipes there began to appear with Turkish names. The Ottoman Empire existed for several centuries when Greece was dominated by the Turks. During this extended period as one civilization and culture replaced another, the cuisine evolved and the names of recipes were changed. Most of the traditional Greek dishes, at times slightly altered by the passing of time, were given foreign names, such as those of their conquerors. It is only natural that conquerors who occupy a country for centuries should leave their mark upon the host country.

That is why so many of the traditional Greek recipes are similar to those of Italy, Turkey, and other neighbors of the Mediterranean. The 2,500 year old ancient Hellenic cuisine evolved through the civilizations from Alexandra the Great though Roman, Byzantine, Italian, and Turkish cultures, along with the invasion of Huns from the north, the Dark Ages, Crusades, Renaissance, and on to modern times.

All of this Mediterranean cuisine is reflected in the food choices at my home in California, where it has become our traditional weekend cuisine. Ahead of an Italian meal of pasta, we will have ante pasta of green onions, radishes, celery, tomatoes, and mushrooms dipped in a saucer of olive oil and vinegar. I learned to make spaghetti sauce from my Italian father-in-law. My Greek son-in-law cooks his souvlaki on a spit with chunks of lamb, or makes his gyro with the same ingredients as shish kebab but wraps them in pita bread together with tzatziki sauce. I discovered shish kebab from an Armenian friend who made it with marinated lamb cut into strips on a skewer, interspersed with slices of onion, tomatoes, and mushrooms. I obtained my skewers from a street vendor in Istanbul, Turkey, and each time I use them I am carried back again to the traditions of the Bosporus. My shish kebab is always served with the rice pilaf that is common to all the countries of that region both in name and composition. From a local deli I can bring home my favorite dessert, the Greek baklava. All these new traditions of my family come from the Mediterranean, and they add much to a pleasant way of life in the modern world.

In conclusion, what goes around comes around again. What started as Greek cuisine in Ancient Greece has recycled back again to modern times with virtually the same recipes, but with Greek, Turkish, Byzantine, and Italian names. Like many of the languages of the modern world such as Latin, French, and English that evolved from the Greek language, so have many of our modern recipes of the Western World that also evolved over the centuries from Ancient Greece.

Treci and George Dimas wedding in 1984 in Toledo, Ohio. At the time, Treci was a Lieutenant, USN, stationed at the communications facility in Norfolk Virginia, and George came as an emigrant from Greece to America as an electrician.

TWENTY SEVEN: *COQ AU VIN*

AH! SWEET MYSTERY OF LIFE [20]

Ah! Sweet mystery of life at last I've found thee
Ah! At last I know the secret of it all;
All the longing, seeking, striving, waiting, yearning.
The idle hopes, the joys and burning tears that fall.
For 'tis love, and love alone, the world is seeking.
And its love and love alone, I've waited for.
And my heart has the answer to its calling.
For it is love that rules forever more.

This song, *Ah! Sweet Mystery of Life,* became a huge hit a hundred years
ago when the operetta *NAUGHTY MARIETTA opened* on Broadway in
1910, and it became a hit with me when I first heard it in the movie with
that same name that starred Jeanette MacDonald and Nelson Eddy.
That was in 1935, when I was a kid living during the Depression in a
poverty-stricken, boring little town that had no glamour; and Jeanette
lifted me up into the new, wondrous world of music – and love. The song
was lofty, beautiful, and it raised my spirits. As a six-year old bachelor, I
had a crush on Jeanette, but it was a neglected love since she never made
it for a visit to see me in Buffalo Gap.

The setting for the operetta was long ago in New Orleans with pirates and swashbuckling heroes, who saved ladies in distress. I don't know why it became so popular, since the lyrics are a bit stilted – thee? -- and certainly dated; but the lofty message was a fit with the beautiful melody composed by Victor Herbert. His songs ruled the charts for several decades, before there even were charts.

Starting with the popular team of Jeanette MacDonald and Nelson Eddy in 1935, the song became a must in the repertoire of many others, including: Bing Crosby, Mario Lanza, Gordon McRae, and even Cloris Leachman, who sang it in an operetta medley with a chorus of pigs in a Muppet show. I don't think the song ever drew the attention of the Beatles, but I'm sure Elvis could have made it into a big hit if the lyrics had reached Memphis.

Now, at this point I am starting with a rather crude attempt at a segue (According to Webster – "segue": to proceed from one musical number to another -- but TV personalities use it as a maneuver to get to whatever new subject they want to introduce).

We all love a mystery. This is particularly true if it is a secret that is now discovered and it makes us cheerful and happy. Or if it is a mystery with enough variety that it really is a mysterious.

Let me set the stage. My wife's ancestry is Italian and her family particularity loves a mystery and almost everything had to be revealed by way of a surprise: a surprise birthday party, a camouflaged Christmas present, or even a surprise at the dinner table. When it is a mystery or surprise, the occasion is elevated by ten-fold.

End of segue; I have arrived. There it is, a mystery package resting on the center of your plate when you sit down to dinner. Since my wife is 100% Italian and my four children are all 50%, a mystery meal is always one of their favorite meals, regardless of what is inside. Even though they have a pretty good idea of what is coming, they are never certain because of two things: there is always something different than last time, and it is hidden from view until the moment when the surprise is unveiled.

Here is how to prepare it; this is not complicated, so no need to take notes.

Cut a 12 inch square piece of aluminum foil on the kitchen counter, one for each person. On top of it place a mixture of favorite vegetables (or those you want the kids to eat): carrots, broccoli, cauliflower, potatoes, mushrooms, boiler onions, or shallots (shallots? only kidding!). Add salt and pepper, and butter and some water. Now here is the important ingredient, and it can vary from one time to the next. On top of the vegetable place one jumbo hot dog. Carefully wrap the package tightly, and place it on the hot grill or in the oven. (Remember, aluminum foil cannot go in the microwave.) Remove the package from the grill in 20 minutes and let it "rest" until time to eat. Call everyone to dinner where they find this mystery package sitting in the middle of their plate.

Now, it is important to conduct a guessing contest for a little fun before the packages are opened. Maybe a prize dessert for the person making the correct guess (however, everyone should get a dessert, so a pall does not fall over the event).

The first time use a hot dog. Then each time, try something else like a bratwurst, turkey hot dog, chicken wing, drumstick, or different and new vegetables. Here is a subtle way to introduce new things to the family with "an offer they can't refuse."

Here is my latest creation, and it is good enough for entertaining family friends (who have a sense of humor). It is my version of *coq au vin*. The guests will never suspect what is inside the package. It will include one chicken thigh, potato, carrots, leeks, and two mushrooms.

Since all these ingredients do not require the same amount of time to cook, you will need to precook a couple of them in the microwave. Zap the cut up potato and carrots for 3 minutes and the thigh for 5 minutes.

Lay a 14x14 inch square of aluminum foil on a plate. On it place the pre-cooked thigh, potato, carrots, cut-up leeks, mushrooms, and butter. Finely chop some parsley and sprinkle over the top, and salt and pepper. Now here is what makes it coq au vin. Over the chicken pour one ounce of brandy and two ounces of a wine (I use pinot noir). Tightly fold the aluminum foil around the creation. Then lay a second sheet of aluminum on the plate and invert the creation and again tightly fold, then repeat this process a third time to create an air tight package and one that will not leak as you turn it over from time to time while cooking. Aluminum foil is inexpensive.

Place the mystery package in the oven (on a pan) at 350 degrees for 20 minutes, inverting the package a time or two. Remove the package from the oven and let it rest for 20 minutes before the guests open them. If you are doing this on a grill while camping as I often do, then cooking may take longer, depending on the heat of the fire.

I plan to serve this tonight at dinner for a special occasion with my wife and some guests, but please keep it a secret so my wife will be surprised.

Ah! Sweet mystery, at last I've found thee.

These are two cowboy oil paintings of mine. The one on the previous page is *Cowboy in the Barn*, and this one is *After a Hard Day's work*.

I am not a good painter and I have never had a lesson, but I find it an enjoyable pastime -- better than golf, but not as good as tennis.

TWENTY EIGHT: I DID IT MY WAY

... I've lived a life that's full
I've travelled each and ev'ry highway
And more, much more than this,
I did it my way. [21]

I was recently listening to a concert by the Dutch conductor, Andre Rieu. During a conversational break in the concert, he said that Frank Sinatra was the world's most popular singer. I don't know if that's true, but he was certainly a great singer and one of my favorites for my entire adult life from the time that Frank first sang on the weekly show, the Hit Parade.

As I listened to a medley of his songs, I was carried back fifty years to the occasion when Aurdery and I shared a cocktail with Frank and his date, Juliet Prose.

Aurdery and I were vacationing with her extended family in a cabin at Lake Tahoe. Her brother, Hank, had rented a large cabin and invited his father and mother, two aunts, and Aurdery and I to stay the weekend. Hank made the suggestion to Aurdery and I that we should take advantage of using him as a babysitter, and go to some casino and party. It sounded good to us, so we did.

Cal-Neva was a beautiful resort on the north shore of Lake Tahoe where it straddled the state line between California and Nevada. The half of the resort on the Nevada side was a gaming casino. At that particular time, the resort was in the headlines for something even more spectacular: Frank Sinatra was rumored to be part owner. Frank was notorious for keeping friends who were rumored to have connections to the Mafia. Of course that raised the hackles of the Nevada State Gaming Commission, which controlled all gambling in the state. Any connection of a casino owner to a member of the mob would be an automatic disqualification for a gaming license. All this saga was spread across the headlines around the nation.

Since Aurdery and I had a free evening to party, where better than at the Cal-Neva Resort. We entered a big reception area just inside the main entrance and found it over-flowing with hundreds of people packed shoulder-to-shoulder. We forced our way in and slowly picked our way through the crowd, looking for some celebrity. The "rat pack" of Sinatra's friends would surely be there. We saw nothing of Dean Martin, or Sammy Davis Junior. Suddenly, Aurdrey saw a famous person: Joe E Lewis, a comedian and close friend of Sinatra. She was excited, grabbed me, and pointed him out to me. As she was backing up to get a better look, she stumbled and nearly knocked the person behind her off his feet. I turned to help him; it was Frank Sinatra.

I don't recall the apologies and forgiving discussion that took place, but we were embarrassed and decided to exit the room and head to the bar. We found the bar virtually empty, because everyone was in the reception area with Frank. There were empty stools, so we took them, sat down, and ordered a drink. Who should walk into the bar and take stools beside us but Frank Sinatra and his squeeze, Juliet Prowse.

"Bartender, I'll have an old fashioned, if you please," he said. He and I sat side by side and ignored each other. Juliet Prowse sat looking bored. By this time, the entire bar area had filled up shoulder-to-shoulder. Finally, it was time for the floor show to begin in the showroom, so

Frank got up and escorted Juliet in that direction. They were followed by virtually everyone in the bar. Apparently, everyone there, except for Aurdrey and me, were part of his entourage. We were left alone in an empty bar.

"Bartender, I'll have an old fashioned, if you please," I said. I've been drinking them every since. If there were good enough for Frank Sinatra, they were good enough for me.

Aurdery's younger brother, Richard (Dick) Castello

Aurdery's oldest brother, Dr. Henry (Hank) Castello

The three Fresno girls: Nona, Aurdery, and Baby Louise

TWENTY NINE: MY RELIGIOUS LANDSCAPE

My first job was working as a cowboy on the 7-11 ranch west of Buffalo Gap. Unlike the glamour portrayed by Hollywood, it was a tough and lonely life; a hard day's work was followed by the loneliness of a night watching campfire embers die. Badger Clark, poet laureate of South Dakota, was a cowboy during his early years. Here are some lines from a poem he wrote about that life.

A COWBOY'S PRAYER [22]

Oh Lord, I've never lived where churches grow.
I love creation better as it stood
That day You finished it so long ago
And looked upon Your work and called it good

I know that others find You in the light
That's sifted down through tinted window panes,
And yet I seem to feel You near tonight
In this dim quiet starlight on the plains

My religious education was ecumenical as a result of parents who came from different religions and lived in rural communities, where differences were kept on a back burner. My father was raised in a Catholic environment, so we went to that church every third Sunday when a missionary priest came to town; on the second Sunday my mother took us to Methodist Sunday school; and on other Sundays we got our religious education with family picnics in the fresh air and sunshine up in the meadows of the Black Hills. I'm not sure which experience had the biggest impact on my life, but I think the latter.

Ten years ago, prior to the 9/11 Twin Towers Disaster, I published a book on religion and was joined by five co-authors who were religious leaders: a Muslim scholar, Jewish rabbi, Catholic priest, Protestant minister, and Buddhist Minister. Our book, *RIDING THE FENCE LINES: Riding the Fences That Define the Margins of Religious Tolerance*, received much praise, and some of this was because we tackled such a difficult and controversial subject and apparently placed it in proper perspective. I wrote chapters about each religion as it was described in non-secular history books, and then each religious leader described how they came to their faith and what they believed in.

The following year, the 9/11 disaster occurred and in the decade since then the religious landscape has dramatically changed within the United States and world-wide. We are witnessing a religious revolution, perhaps the most significant one during the five centuries since the reformation. Some of the changes are no-doubt the result of 9/11, while others reflect changes as we undergo a modern cultural revolution. Let me describe some of the things that are happening, and most of these are supported by various polls.

The biggest religious challenge is conflict between the Christian and the Islamic world, and even changes within the latter as extremist Muslims move further to the right, while mainstream Muslims look for a middle ground that is compatible with the multi-religious populations where they live. The struggle is too muddled to predict where it is headed or will end -- if it ever does. In former years, the Christian and

165

Muslims populations were held apart by national boundaries, but now there is no separation in a global melting pot where populations are intermixed, and there is now the added dimension of Christian armies fighting inside Muslim countries.

In addition, other major changes are occurring in the religious landscape.

The Roman Catholic Church has seen a decline in membership with young adults. That decline is now acerbated by the exposure of decades of sexual abuses by priests on a world-wide scale. This exodus from the church is most evident in its home base of Europe, where cathedrals and churches sit nearly empty, attended only by older people, widows and tourists. The Vatican is attempting to reverse the decline with new out-reach to Hispanic and Black populations in the United States, South America and Africa.

The decline in religious affiliation is most evident in mainline Protestant churches, where membership decreased from seventeen to twelve percent in the past seven years, according to the polls. [23] That is, indeed, a dramatic drop. It is underscored by the realization that for the first time in the history of our nation, we do not have a single Protestant justice on the Supreme Court, which is now composed of 6 Roman Catholics and three ethnic Jews.

No discussion of religion is complete unless one also looks at the communities of non-believers, which contain nearly one-fourth of all Americans. According to recent polls, nearly a quarter of Americans fit in the category of non-believers. [24] This includes fifteen percent who say they have no religion and another twelve percent who may believe in a higher power but not in a personal God -- the core belief of monotheistic faiths such as Judaism, Christianity and Islam. [25] This number of non-believers is nearly twice the size of the mainline Protestant church population.

The credibility of religious polls is questionable because some people dissemble, hedge, and are not forthright in revealing their true religious beliefs; however, recent trends indicate people are moving away from religious practice and belief in a God, or else they are now "coming out of the closet." During past times, it has sometimes been a social kiss of death to admit to being an agnostic or an atheist. It is similar to the trend we see that men and women will now openly acknowledge they are gay.

Buddhism membership appears to be on the increase, perhaps because it is less doctrinaire. Rather than looking outward to a personal God, one looks inward to within their self and psychic. A Buddhist is free to accept a wide range of religious beliefs.

The Eastern Orthodox religion seems to be on the rebound overseas as the vast regions of Russia have thrown off the atheistic doctrines of communism and returned to their Christian roots.

Over the long course of history, the ebb and flow of religions through populations has varied during such times as wars, famines, natural disasters, and global cultural changes. The trends we see today could all be reversed in the future, but don't count on it. As people become better educated, populations more literate, science more widely understood, superstition and witchcraft less prevalent, and world-wide communication improved, it appears that these factors all help motivate the religious cultural changes we see today.

Having been raised as a part-time Protestant in my youth, I feel comfortable when I attend their Evangelical services. Is my Protestant God the same one I pray to in my Catholic Church? Does the same God serve all the religious faiths and also the infidels with no faith? Is our Christian God, Yahweh, the same guy as Jehovah of Judaism, and Allah of the Muslims? If not, then He must be a strange God to exclude so many. Which of us are left stranded and hopeless on the parapet? If they are all the same God; then He must be sad to see people squabbling over dogma; fighting about a protocol for worship.

Ad COLELUM

At the Muezzin's call for prayer,
The kneeling faithful thronged the square,
And on Pushkara's lofty height
The dark priest chanted Brahmin's might.
Amid a monastery's weeds
An old Franciscan told his beads,
While to the synagogue there came
A Jew, to praise Jehovah's name.
The one great God looked down and smiled
And counted each His loving child;

For Turk and Brahmin, monk and Jew
Had reached Him through the Gods they knew. [26]

We each must ultimately reach beyond the confines of our inherited culture to resolve the riddle of life's meaning; make this hardest of all journeys -- the search for a God -- by ourselves; and find it within our own frail being. After I left the cowboy culture I inherited and traveled through the outside world, I encountered the dogmas and mores of other cultures and religious traditions that have evolved into armed camps through centuries of conflict. Riding Those Fence Lines has been a tough day's work.

ENDNOTES

1. *THE REST OF THE WORLD GO BY*, Written in 1919, lyrics by J. Keirn Brennan, music by Ernest R. Ball. Text is available under the Creative Commons Attribution-ShareAlike License.
2. Olcott and Graff, music by Ball, *The Isle O'Dreams*, 1912
3. Dee Brown, *Bury My Heart At Wounded Knee*, Holt Rinehart, NY, 1971, p. 297, in the public domain
4. *REMEMBER PEARL HARBOR*, Words by Don Reid and music by Reid and Sammy Kaye, Copyright 1941 by Republic Music Corporation, 607 Fifth Avenue, New York, NY. Text is available under the Creative Commons Attribution-ShareAlike License.
5. *YOU ARE MY SUNSHINE*, by Jimmie Davis, Copyright 1940, by Peer International Corporation, Copyright renewed, All rights reserved. Used by Permission
6. *LONG AGO AND FAR AWAY*, Lyrics by Ira Gershwin, music by Jerome Kern, Copyright 1944 by Columbia Pictures, Burbank, CA. Text is available under the Creative Commons Attribution-ShareAlike License.

7. *THE SWEETHEART OF SIGMA CHI,* written by Byron D. Stokes and F. Dudleigh Vernor, copyright 1911, Edward & Verna Publishing Co. NY

8. *I'LL BE HOME FOR CHRISTMAS,* music by Walter Kent, copyright 2010, AMG (All Media Guide). Text is available under the Creative Commons Attribution-ShareAlike License.

9. *TENDERLY,* music by Walter Gross and lyrics by Jack Lawrence.Copyright 1946 by Edwin H. Morris Company, Inc. Text is available under the Creative Commons Attribution-ShareAlike License.

10. *I REMEMBER IT WELL,* Lyrics by ALAN JAY LERNER, music by FREDERICK LOEWE, copyright 1958, Alfred Publishing Co. PO Box 10003, Van Nuys, CA. By permission.

11. By James Russell Lowell, American Romantic Poet, from his epic poem, *The Vision of Sir Launfal,* in the public domain.

12. *O SOLE MIO,* written in 1909, usually sung in the original Neapolitan language, in the public domain.

13. "Mediterranean Cuisine," *Winipeda the Free Encyclopedia,* 2010

14. Chrissa Paradissis, *The Best Book of Greek Cookery,* Efstalhiadis Group SA, Attika, Greece, 1993

15. Ibid, p. 10

16. Ibid, p. 11

17. Ibid, p. 14

18. Ibid, p. 14

19. Ibid, p. 15

20. *AH! SWEET MYSTERY OF LIFE,* Copyright 1910 in operetta *NAUGHTY MARIETTA,* in the public domain.

21. *I DID IT MY WAY*, lyrics by Paul Anka, copyright 1968. Text is available under the Creative Commons Attribution-ShareAlike License.

22. Badger Clark, Sun and Saddle Leather, Chapman & Grimes, 1935, in the public domain.

23. Rachel Zoll, AP Religion Writer, Yahoo News, 2/9/2009

24. Ib id

25. Eliza Gray, Newsweek, 5/13/2009, p. 34

26. *The Best Loved Poems of the American People*, Doubleday, 1936 A poem by Harry Romaine, In the public domain.

Manufactured By: RR Donnelley
                     Momence, IL USA
                     January, 2011